The Telegraph BUSINESS CLUB

STRATEGY AND PERFORMANCE

The Telegraph
BUSINESSCLUB
STRATEGY
AND
PERFORMANCE

James B. Rieley

Hodder Arnold

www.hoddereducation.co.uk

For UK order enquiries: please contact Bookpoint Ltd, 130 Milton Park, Abingdon, Oxon OX14 4SB. Telephone: +44 (0) 1235 827720. Fax: +44 (0) 1235 400454. Lines are open 09.00–18.00, Monday to Saturday, with a 24-hour message answering service. Details about our titles and how to order are available at www.hoddereducation.com

British Library Cataloguing in Publication Data: a catalogue record for this title is available from the British Library.

ISBN-10: 0 340 91397 5
ISBN-13: 9 780340 91397 5

First published in UK 2006 by Hodder Education, 338 Euston Road, London, NWI 3BH in association with The Telegraph Business Club.

This edition published 2006.

Typeset by Servis Filmsetting Limited, Longsight, Manchester
Printed in Great Britain for Hodder Education, a division of Hodder Headline, 338 Euston Road, London NW1 3BH, by Bath Press Ltd, Bath

Hodder Headline's policy is to use papers that are natural, renewable and recyclable products and made from wood grown in sustainable forests. The logging and manufacturing processes are expected to conform to the environmental regulations of the country of origin.

Impression number   10 9 8 7 6 5 4 3 2 1

Year   2011 2010 2009 2008 2007 2006

Performance without a strategy is a function of luck;
strategy without performance is the result of incompetence.

contents

preface

Strategy and performance are usually thought of as the realm of the big consultancies. Yes, many of them have done some pretty serious work in these areas, but it has always amazed me that whilst they bring high-powered consultants to bear for clients, many with the latest and greatest tools and methodologies, many of their efforts fail. And fail dismally.

There seems to be something lacking within all the tools and methodologies; and that something is *common sense*. Too often, companies from all sectors find out that their massive investments in strategic consultants do not bring the results they are after. And, as a result, they go back to their consultants and ask for more. This in itself seems to be lacking in common sense.

On the other hand, there are companies who, with or without consultants, are able to craft strategies that do deliver performance. And the one common element that is visible in all these companies is that they test their strategies consistently with common sense.

When asked by the publishers to write this book, my first thought was to see what was already written about strategy and performance. So, where did I look? Amazon.com seemed to be the logical place to check and, according to Amazon, they offer 14,121 books on strategy and 23,885 books on performance. Okay, so this isn't exactly a new topic, but it did cause me to wonder: if there are so many books out there, why is it that companies still struggle with the topics? Is it that management is not able to read? Is it that they just don't get it? Or are there so many books on these topics because everyone thinks they are experts? Well, I am not an expert on strategy or on performance. But, I am someone who has seen pretty much of what has been done in these areas in my time as CEO and as senior management advisor. And what I have seen is not pretty. But, as my publisher wanted me to do this book, I realised I was faced with a choice: I could either fill the pages with trendy, state-of-the-art methodologies and tools; or focus the content on common sense ways that a company's management can use to make sure that their strategy *can work* and, when it does, will deliver sustainable high performance. And do it in plain talk.

I wasn't told to put together the thickest business book ever made. But I was asked to write a book that, in plain talk, explains how organisations can realise their potential by having a common-sense strategy that can improve organisational performance.

This book is not rocket science. And, as many of you may discern, it doesn't even contain the latest and greatest trendy insights about strategy and performance. What it does do is provide useful, practical, common sense information for managers who want and need to get their respective acts together to develop and implement a strategy that works; and, with it, achieve sustainable high performance.

Dr James B. Rieley
jbrieley@rieley.com
www.rieley.com

With appreciation to

Daniel Kim,
for inspiring so much of this work;

Ian Clarkson,
who helped me get my head around what
performance is all about;

Richard Collins,
for constant reality checks;

Alison Frecknall and John Hudson,
for believing;

Richard Smith,
for always sharing and encouraging
common sense;

Gabriel Kow,
for his insights and many contributions on
how to turn around performance;

Angelina,
for always being with me;

and

all those friends and associates who have
provided stories
and editorial support for this project.

Introduction

Well, I don't know about you, but I am getting a bit tired of reading all the stories in the business media about companies today. Well, that is not exactly right. What I am tired of is the seemingly constant use of buzzwords, trendy terms, flashy fads, academic theories and metaphors to explain why companies are performing the way they are. I am also tired of reading about all the excuses why the performance that has been demonstrated by business in the past years is not the fault of the people running the companies.

You may or may not agree with me, but I think it is about time to start using plain talk to explain what is going on in the business world. This book is just that – a book using plain talk to explain how companies can develop more comprehensive strategies – strategies that actually work – and so to deliver sustainable performance over time.

Business is all about making money. I know that some companies have mission statements that make wonderful references to glorious missions using words that are usually full of references that reflect the times. But the bottom line is that the main reason that businesses exist is to make money. Period. To make money, a business has to do one thing – perform well. In most cases, at least in the cases in which there are two or more companies doing the same thing, performing well means that the company has to perform better than its competition.

> **Think what you will, but business is all about making money. Period.**

I find it really interesting that although every CEO and senior manager knows that their first job is to deliver results in terms of money, they still banter mission statements about that speak of innovative ways to do what they do; creative initiatives that focus on some magnificent challenge, or some generic set of words that mean almost anything to anyone. So why is it that we don't hear about the money part? Especially since the business journals all print results that are monetarily focused. It's all about making money. And the best way to do this sustainably is to improve performance based on a strategy that can actually work.

If you are a shareholder of a company, you want it to make money – lots of it – because that is how *you* will make money. The more money they make, the more money you make. And we all talk about the money part, but are we prepared to admit to ourselves that the money is really what motivates us?

Read any interview of a CEO and you will see what I mean. Sure, he (CEOs are rarely women nowadays, which is another whole issue that needs to be changed but, none-the-less, I will use 'he' to reference CEOs from here on in) may talk about his company's market share – a veiled reference to the company's ability to make lots of money; he may talk about capital investments – a veiled reference to spending money on equipment or facilities so the company can make money faster with less cost; he may talk about human resources – a veiled reference to how much money is being spent on having people work in the company; or he may talk about all the glorious things they do to make our lives better – a veiled reference to how much money they will get because we like what they do. But I can't remember the last time I read an interview in which the CEO openly stated that the main purpose of his company was to make lots of money. This is especially fascinating, because this is how the CEO gets paid. Just think about this for a minute. If the company makes lots of money, the CEO usually makes lots of money. Rarely do we hear about CEOs who are paid based on how clever their employees are; rarely do we hear about CEOs who are paid based on how clever they are – the bottom line is that CEOs are paid based on how much money the company makes. And if the company doesn't make lots of money, the CEO is chucked out and a new one is brought in who will. That is the way it works.

Now I am not saying that making money is bad. The reality is that companies have to make money to be able to pay their employees, to buy new machines or equipment so the employees can work, buy buildings so the employees have a place to work, and invest in advertising so potential customers know how they can spend their money. What bugs me is that we don't seem to be open to facing up to it.

Okay, so let's move on a bit. If the challenge is to make money, how can a company do this in the best possible way? Well, as I said earlier, the best way to do this is to consistently deliver performance. And companies really aren't too consistent with this. There are quite a few reasons for this. Delivering performance consistently from year to year requires a couple of things, some of which are pretty obvious, and some aren't so obvious. Business performance is a bit like a mathematics equation and most people think the equation looks like this. To get consistent performance, you need to have the right people, who clearly understand what is expected of them, who have the right skills and the right equipment, and who are committed to what needs to be done. And it needs a sound plan on how they are going to accomplish all this.

With me so far? So what do you suppose happens when a company doesn't perform as well as it can? You hit it right on the head. If you believe some pretty well-recognised CEOs who have been in the media in the past 20 or so years, the problem is that one or more elements of this equation are missing. Take Roger Smith, for example. Remember in the late 1970s? Roger Smith was the head of General Motors and at the time good ol' GM was getting hammered by the Japanese car industry. I remember hearing Mr Smith in a news conference explaining why this was happening, and his explanation was incredible. Yes, the Japanese car industry was racking up monster sales in America, and this was causing devastating performance results for GM. And the reason was that (paraphrasing Smith), 'the Japanese were selling too many cars in America'. I found this fascinating at the time (and still do), largely because I was driving a Toyota wagon. Nice car. When I heard what Smith was using as his defence for poor company performance, I thought to myself that his statements were way off base. Sure, I was driving a Japanese car, but not because it was sold to me. I was driving a Japanese car because the American car companies just weren't making cars that I wanted to buy. They cost more, they had more quality problems, they didn't last as long, they got worse mileage and they didn't look as good. I was driving a Japanese car because I bought one, not because someone sold one to me. Now you may think that this is just a word game, but think about it a little harder. When was the last time that you 'bought' something? Did you buy it because you wanted it, or did you buy it because someone sold it to you?

Well, Roger Smith's argument didn't sit well with the clever business journal writers who honed in on the fact that GM cars (and most American cars at the time) cost more because the workers who made them were paid more than their counterparts in Japan. The quality of the American cars wasn't as good as

Japanese cars because the factories in which the employees worked were old and out of date. Good points, but I think that the reason the Japanese car companies were able to do so much better than American car companies was that the heads of the American car companies had lost the plot. They just weren't doing their jobs of delivering consistent performance year after year.

> **Many American companies had lost the plot and weren't giving customers what they wanted.**

Most certainly, they knew that they were supposed to make lots of money, but they definitely didn't know how to make good decisions, nor did their direct reports, obviously. They didn't understand what American car consumers thought was really important. They didn't understand that there was a major competitive threat out there. And they didn't understand that to motivate employees to be highly productive takes more than just telling them to work harder and paying them more. So, think back to that time . . . who took the hit for the failures of General Motors? Well, the employees who lost their jobs to the competition took a hit. The other companies who would have done better had there been more American workers keeping their jobs and getting paid so they could spend their money, and you and I, because if we didn't shift our buying habits to buy what we really wanted, things cost more while, at the same time, we received less. Oh yes, Mr Smith eventually did lose his job at General Motors, but I don't think he suffered too much – he was given some incredible bonus of millions of dollars for being a 'good leader'. What a load of rubbish. The biggest real reason that GM lost the battle with Japanese car makers was that the company didn't have a workable strategy.

There is a lot of evidence of this. First, they must not have been able to think out the issues that they were facing. If they could have, they wouldn't have let the company get into the mess it found itself. They must not have been able to influence and motivate employees to make a competitive product, or consumers to keep buying it. They must not have been able to lead the company by making sure that the employees had the necessary equipment and facilities to be competitive. And they must not have been able to achieve what they needed to do, as can be seen from their performance. The problems experienced by GM were due to the lack of sound management and leadership on the part of the highest paid people in the company. This doesn't need to happen to you and your company. If you are serious, and I mean really serious, about improving your performance and that of your company, read on.

I have always had beliefs about strategy and performance. One belief is that they go hand in hand. You cannot deliver consistent, sustainable performance without a strategy that has this as one of its focus areas. Performance – that is serious high performance – does not occur just because you want it to. Performance happens because you *make it happen*; and to make it happen, you need to have a strategy for it.

Another belief is that most strategies are lame. Well, that may not be exactly right; I think that most strategies just don't really make the connection between what the company wants to accomplish and what the people are competent to do. They aren't based on reality, they don't focus on what the organisation is trying to achieve, and they aren't doable. In short, they are not common sense.

Years ago, I worked at a higher educational institution after coming out of retirement the first time. Working at a college certainly was different than owning your own business, and my new colleagues let me know that every day. I had been hired to develop a concept that would drive continuous quality improvement in the institution. The challenge was a bit tall at the time, as the faculty – this was a highly unionised environment – believed that they *did not have customers*. Not having customers or at least believing that they didn't have customers, was an interesting concept, especially for me, coming from over 20 years in manufacturing.

After getting this concept I was hired to develop up and running, I was called to the President's office. I was being asked to 'take over' the college's strategic planning process, largely because the college's accreditation was coming up and I had many years' experience running a successful business, and – these are the words used by the President – *'if you lead it, we can include all that quality s**t you do. The accreditation agency will love it'.*

I had seen the previous two strategic plans earlier, and what impressed me was that they were fabulous . . . well, they *looked* fabulous. The last one had been printed in four colours, laid out on A3 paper; but printed horizontally, so it looked like a set of architectural plans. The cover said something like 'building our future'. Cute. But inside, there was little that was strategic about them. Lots of goals and initiatives that appeared to have been picked out of the sky; no apparent accountabilities for getting things done; and no clear ways to measure success; no information about how or why the chosen goals were selected; and no way to know if the plan would even work. But it did have lots of great looking pictures.

Developing a strategy for any type of organisation follows the same basic rules. Whether the organisation is a manufacturer, a service organisation, from the health-care sector, from the IT sector, from the higher education sector, or from government, the rules are all the same – understand where you are, where you want to go, what the future might bring, and how best to get where you want to go.

A strategy should be like a very visible roadmap that anyone can clearly understand. It is the plan that will be used to take an organisation into the future. But part of getting to the future implies (or should imply) that there is a future that the organisation *wants to get to*; as well as a sense of what may or may not occur on the strategic journey. If a strategy doesn't have these two things, it might as well be written with invisible ink, because that is what it is probably worth.

The Institute of Directors recently released the results of a study they commissioned to see how much effort businesses were putting into getting ready for the future. When I read some of the study results, I was floored. Sixty-nine per cent of the respondents to the question, *'what factors inhibit future thinking in your organisation'* stated that they were *'too busy'*. Too busy to figure out what the future might bring? Wake up, lads; the light at the end of the tunnel just may be an oncoming train.

> **There are two important words that differentiate a strategy from an effective strategy: common sense.**

According to the report, 30 per cent of the respondents mentioned that they had *'a lack of in-house expertise'*, and another 31 per cent sited *'inadequate resources'* as the reason that their ability to see into the future was inhibited. These responses raise a very serious question – how can organisations expect to survive into the future when no one is trying to determine what that future might bring?

Yes, managers today are probably busier than ever, but busy doing what? Most of the managers I speak to seem to have their diaries filled with ongoing, recurring problems that have never been really solved. They are inundated with assignments and responsibilities that feed the addiction to reactive thinking and fire fighting. Just look at the stories in the media: budget airlines that don't seem to care if they alienate customers because they assume that other customers will fill the seats; energy company managers who are so busy patting themselves on the back for high profits that they forget it wasn't their decision-making excellence that generated them, but instead the global demand for oil; and senior managers who are quick to say their heads are on the line, but then shun the responsibility for organisational performance. It might be time for shareholders to press for more accountability for the future of business.

The ability or, in many cases, willingness to look to the future can be a make or break competency for companies. Behaviours and skills that were acceptable a dozen years ago just don't cut it nowadays. Being 'too busy' to try to put clarity on potential scenarios that a business may face is akin to driving your car at high speed day and night, just to rack up as many miles as possible. Sure, you may see your odometer climb quickly, but if you don't stop once in a while to check the engine or put petrol in, you will end up sitting on the side of the road watching your competitor cruise past. To put it plainly, there simply is no excuse for not trying to understand what the future might bring unless, of course, you don't care. And in some companies I know, that is the case.

The average tenure in a senior organisational position today is declining. CEOs seem to last as long as summer in England and when the new one arrives, the first piece of business appears to be how to make his mark on the company. That behaviour is almost understandable; they are given high-paying jobs with lots of responsibility and are under pressure to deliver the performance results the last guy apparently wasn't able to deliver. But seldom do we see new leaders begin by focusing on ensuring that the business will survive long after they have retired. Instead, the focus is on driving short-term results that distract from the larger issue of sustainability.

Over 30 years ago, the people at Royal Dutch Shell did planning based not only on what they needed to accomplish, but also on *what might happen in the future*. They were the only energy company that had plans ready to deal with what we know now as OPEC. And these plans enabled them to be prepared when the price of crude oil skyrocketed. They were thinking in terms far longer than the literal tomorrow. Unfortunately, this ability within Shell has disappeared, as they now, as we have seen, seem to have had a focus on managing the market expectations through number manipulation. The story of GEC-Marconi is another prime example. When Lord Weinstock was the head of GEC, the company kept thinking about what the future might bring. No, it wasn't sexy and cool to do that, but the company was profitable and stable and postured for the future. And then Weinstock was sent away and new people came in who were blinded by the immediate future. And as shareholders of Marconi can attest, the once proud company is just a shadow of its previous self, and probably lucky to be in business at all.

If you don't know what the future may hold, you will never get there in one piece.

Does Ryanair really think that they will always have enough customers with their apparent policy of 'do it our way or go find another carrier'? Are the decision makers at BP so sure that the price of oil will never again go down? Do the senior people at BA think that just because they used to be the best, they will always be in business? What are these companies going to do if they are wrong? Come on people, let's use some common sense and realise that the future is not guaranteed.

Senior management needs to re-think some of their priorities. Planning for the future is just as important as planning for next quarter, and not having people looking long-term is inexcusable in today's business world. The light at the end of the tunnel could very well be an incoming train.

part I

Strategy

01

Understanding Potential Futures

Developing a set of potential scenarios that your company may encounter

Scenario planning is used to figure out *what might happen* in the future. Scenarios, after all, are possible events and not necessarily what is. Whilst this is something that all organisations should be doing, regardless of size, scope or sector, it is rarely done well, if at all. But that is not what management thinks. Planning for the future is something that almost every organisation believes that it does. We plan on how many customers we will have in the future; we plan on what our revenues will be in the future; we plan on what profit levels we will attain; we plan on what the impact will be of new innovative ways to do what we do. We plan what our budgets will be for the next year. Sometimes, we plan on what our technology needs will be for the next two years. This is planning for the literal future, you know, the next year or two; but not for the real future. The future that we need to look at is the future that will become today in 10, 20 or 30 years.

> **Planning for the future is something that almost every organisation believes that it does, but the reality is that they don't.**

Many organisations have been plodding along for many years without having to deal with what the future might bring. But today, they are going through massive changes. Their customers are changing, their competition is changing, their customer's needs are changing and their resource availability is changing. The world of business is taking shape in not only new, but in entirely different ways. If they are to remain viable, and hopefully more effective over time, all organisations must begin to examine how they do their planning.

When we do our planning for the 'immediate future', the future of one or two years away, we are like someone who is standing in the woods against a tree with his or her nose touching the bark. We are able to focus our vision on the crevices on the bark, perhaps even on the small creatures that inhabit the tree lining. Consequently, we begin to believe that our 'world' is the tree bark and the small creatures. However, even trying to focus at this distance requires that we force our eyes to clearly see what is in front of us. Unfortunately, being this close to the tree eliminates our ability to discern how big in diameter the tree is, or how tall the tree is, or how many trees are in the forest. We may not even be able to tell if the tree is diseased and might fall on us at a later date. The mental models we have of our environment become locked into place by our self-enforced myopic position.

Planning for the immediate future runs the same risks. When we look at the future of one or two years, we will not be able to focus on the bigger picture. We need to 'step back from the tree' and focus on the forest as a whole. Scenario planning gives us that ability. Scenario planning is not about doing planning, but is the vehicle in which we can begin to change the mental models we have of our worlds. Organisational survival depends on the ability to detect and adapt to critical changes in the environment. We need to change our mental models of what is and what is not; we need to learn how to better plan for the future; we need to better understand what our futures might be. Part I of the book will put forth a common sense, easy-to-use methodology for doing effective scenario planning.

> **Organisational survival 'depends on the ability to detect and adapt to critical changes in the environment that may impact the company'.**

The development of an effective scenario planning process is basically the same, regardless of what sector an organisation is from. In reality, an example from any sector can be used to help people learn how to identify and develop future scenarios that can be applied when building an effective strategy. For the purposes of this book, I will use an example that was used effectively in a higher education environment. Bear in mind, whilst the examples I will show were used in a college, the *actual process*, when used in business, would be the same.

Scenarios in Higher Education

In higher education, colleges and universities are faced with many potential future scenarios. Whilst I am not aware of any organisation that has only one future scenario, most organisations have multiple scenarios that they might encounter, many of them appearing as almost opposites from each other. For higher education, they could include:

Either:	Or:
Enrolments drop	Enrolments increase
Decreased competition	Increased competition
Economic turndown	Economic upturn
Conflicts within communities	Harmony within communities
Conflicts with accrediting agencies	Long-term accreditation
Facility limitations	Unused facility capacity
Resource availability shrinkage	Surplus funding availability
Anti-education legislation	Federal support for education
Technology advances	Increase in need for basic skills
Reduced need for degreed employees	Increased demand for degrees

Figure 1

There is no right or wrong scenario; there are no good or bad scenarios; there are only potential futures facing our organisations. Selecting the scenarios to look at can be a hit-or-miss process. Few organisations have the resources that would enable them to look at all the potential futures, therefore, selecting one or two to examine becomes a matter of practicality. How to make the selection is the question. The method that works well is interviewing organisational suppliers, customers and employees and business research that applies to the sector you are in.

> There are no good or bad scenarios, only scenarios that need to be understood.

By asking the question, '*what do you think the future holds in store for our organisation?*' a scenario planning team can begin to sort out what futures may be important to look at. By sorting the responses into groups, the team can identify some common characteristics. By using orthogonal axes (see Figure 2), we can develop a method of completing the selection process. After selecting two characteristics that are identified in the interview process, the scenario team determines the opposite characteristics and applies all four to the axes. With the axes completed, the scenario team then begins to develop scenarios for each of the four quadrants.

A key consideration in developing scenarios is the richness of the conversation. There are significant obstacles to this process. They include; overconfidence and intellectual arrogance, anchoring and availability bias. As humans, we tend to overestimate our knowledge and level of understanding.

Traditional delivery	
Increase in need for basic skills	Classes at business sites
Lower entrance skills expected	Classes held at shopping centres
Facility expenses increase	Increase in partnerships
Escalating benefit costs	Higher entrance skills expected
Centralised ————————————	———————————— **Site-based**
Increase in operating expenses	No central campus facility
Labour contract conflicts	Faculty on call
Lack of organisational alignment	Heavy utilisation of ITFS, (internet foreign students)
Difficulty in keeping up	Higher entrance skills required
Alternative delivery	

Figure 2

Overconfidence may make us believe that, because we have been successful in the past, we will be able to lead our organisations successfully into an unknown future. Additionally, we may believe that we know exactly what the future will be. We believe that the future will be basically an extension of the past and, consequently, we anchor our beliefs in what we know now.

Through doing scenario planning, we are not trying to pinpoint specific future events, but looking at the large–scale forces that will be pushing the future into different directions. It is these forces that contribute to the changes that affect our institutions.

Most current planning follows maps that we have that are two dimensional, like roadmaps or terrain maps. Making geographic maps is an honoured art and science, so is the making of organisational maps. However, both of them provide a distorted view of the environment. Geographic maps show the elevations, the distances between places and the topography. An organisational map, in the case of higher education, can show the number of students who enrol, the number of students who complete, the number of students in classes, the trends of business and industry, and the various ways in which we deliver education. However, neither map shows the various uncertainties that relate to the reality that the maps are supposed to reflect.

Geographic maps do not include various elements such as weather, landslides, animals and other people that might restrict one's ability to move across the territory shown on the map. Organisational maps do not traditionally include values, legislative directions and impacts, institutional climate, relationships between departments, or levels of understanding and buy-in. These are all considered to be uncertainties.

> **Reducing uncertainty is critical to success.**

When evaluating relationships between uncertainties, we need to check for internal consistency and plausibility; for example, high visibility and heavy snowdrifts are an implausible combination. By examining the driving forces, we begin to surface the uncertainties that will have a major impact on our ability to understand the potential futures we face.

Driving Forces

The forces to be examined include social, economic, political, environmental and technological. It is these forces that will result in the future we will find ourselves in. We need to look at the context of these forces.

```
SCENARIO DRIVING FORCES

Social Dynamic Forces
    Demographics
    Values
    Lifestyle
    Customer demands

Economic Issue Forces
    Microeconomic trends
    Macroeconomic trends

Political Issue Forces
    Legislation
    Regulatory direction
    Accreditation directions

Environmental Forces
    Ecological movement
    Costs of recycling

Technological Issue Forces
    Innovation
    Technology availability
    Indirect technology impacts
```

Figure 3

By beginning to examine these forces, we can begin to paint a picture of the things that will be affecting the relationships that impact our ability to be effective over time. Once the driving forces are identified, it is important to begin to identify the things that can be predetermined. Predetermined forces are ones that we can identify through direct or indirect relationships. For example, it is relatively easy to predetermine how many students will be attending an intermediate school in a given area by looking at how many students there are in the pipeline to intermediate schools, i.e. how many students are in the primary school system in that area.

Although the two numbers in all probability will not be the same, there will be a correlation. Another example might include the number of students who attend graduate programmes. To find this number, we can start by determining the correlation between the number of students in college programmes at an institution.

There will potentially be quite a few driving forces whose outcomes can be predetermined. Once these are identified, we are left with what are called 'uncertainties'. It is the uncertainties that we need to work to discover. It is the uncertainties that are largely controlled by our mental models.

In scenario planning, we are not trying to predict the future; we are trying to understand the potential futures that we might encounter. This requires being open to these potentials, being open to challenging our mental models of what the future might be.

Mental Models

To better examine our mental models, an effective tool that can be used is a systems map. In a systems map, the relationships between various elemental behaviours are identified, as well as the relationships between them. The outcome of using the tool looks like a very chaotic spider's web, with arrows going from behaviour to behaviour. The arrows help define the relationship between the various behaviours by showing the direction of effect, as well as the impact of that direction (see Figure 4).

In Figure 4, the relationships between behaviours from the example are shown. Keys to look for are the arrow directions and the letter near each arrowhead. The arrow shows which behaviour affects which other behaviours. The letter, either an 'S' or an 'O', shows the direction of the impact of the relationship. If the letter is an 'S', the meaning is that, as one behaviour builds or grows, the other (recipient behaviour) builds or grows as well. If

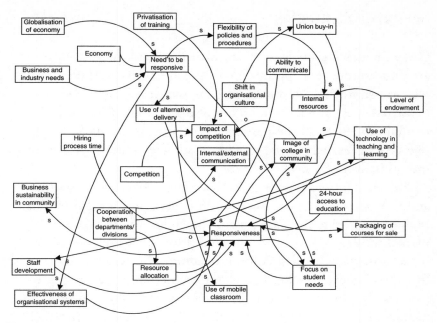

Figure 4

the letter is an 'O', the meaning is that, as one behaviour builds or grows, the other (recipient behaviour) will decline or shrink. By examining the completed systems map, we can determine which behaviours will have the most impact on the system, therefore helping to better understand what may happen in the scenario being looked at.

> **We make decisions based on our mental models about what is good or bad, right or wrong, logical or downright foolish.**

Using a systems map enables us to re-examine our mental models of the relationships at play in our organisations and, in the case of scenario planning, enables us to examine our mental models of how we see the future.

Scenario Strategies

Once the driving behaviours are identified and their relationships are understood, it is appropriate to begin to develop potential scenario strategies. To ensure that the scenario strategies that are constructed are not only valid but also a compilation of the mental models of all the participants, a process should be used that enables varied mental models to surface. This process involves the utilisation of a *scenario matrix*.

This matrix (see Figure 5) is divided into five entry columns and five entry rows, for a total of 25 matrix positions to be filled in. The rows give the participants the ability to articulate their mental models (the beliefs and assumptions that they believe will be congruent with each column heading); the systemic structures that they believe will be present for each column heading; the patterns of behaviour that will be evident for each column heading; and the visible events that will be associated with each column heading. The columns reflect the potential scenario in question, the current reality, the gap between the potential future scenario and the current reality, the action steps identified to help move toward the future scenario, and the indicators of movement toward the future scenario.

The actual process of filling out the matrix is normally completed by individuals, most often by a cross-sectional group of organisational stakeholders. This group, in the case of a college or university, could include students, administrators, faculty and support staff. There is no set way to complete the matrix. Some groups begin horizontally, some begin vertically – the only requirement is that the matrix reflects the vision of the person filling it out.

Once the group has completed their individual matrices, they would begin to build a 'collective' matrix; a matrix that reflects the collective vision of the group members. This process can be quite time consuming, depending on the alignment among the group members and the ability of the group to function as team.

Level of perspective	Potential scenario	Current reality	Gap	Action steps	Indicators
Organisational condition					
Mental models					
Systemic structures					
Patterns of behaviour					
Events					

Figure 5

It is important when developing the collective matrix to identify the target format for each matrix position. The columns for potential scenario and current reality are most suited for sentences, while the columns for gap, action steps and indicators are best suited for bullet points.

The purpose for using the matrix is two-fold. First, it helps to build alignment on the planning team by creating a common knowledge base of what is and what can be. By completing the matrix and sharing the inputs, the team can develop a collective view of the future that is based on the individual perspectives of the group. Second, completing the matrix forces people to deal with three levels of knowledge: 1) things we know we know, 2) things we know we don't know, and 3) things we don't know we don't know. The object of using the matrix is not to validate or invalidate any specific future, but to think through the implications of that future.

Upon completion of the collective matrix, the scenario team would then repeat the process for the other scenarios identified by the orthogonal axes.

> **Understanding the future does not happen overnight.**

During this process, two concerns usually come up. First, a concern about the time and, therefore, the cost, involved. Second, a concern about the relevance of the outcomes. There are no right answers for these concerns. However, when faced with similar concerns in the 1970s when presenting potential scenarios relating to what could happen to the availability of the world's oil supply, Pierre Wack (the founder of scenario planning) responded, we 'need to weigh the probability against the seriousness of the consequence – if it happens, and you are not prepared for it'. As we all remember, the seriousness of the consequence in that scenario was extremely high. In higher education, institutions are faced with future potentials that could have the same level of seriousness of consequence for our organisations if we do not begin to look at our mental models of the future.

Scenario planning is many things. However, it will not give organisations answers. It will not enable us to make better predictions. Scenario planning will give us the opportunity to explore and, perhaps, expand our mental models of what the future could be, and what we can do as it approaches so that we can be better prepared for the challenges it will bring.

Scenario planning is about understanding the futures that might happen. Scenario planning will provide the opportunity to ask the questions that will need to be asked if we are to become better at planning for our future.

Scenario Checklist

1 Does your organisation do scenario planning?
2 How do you identify the potential scenarios that your organisation might encounter?
3 Who in the organisation is involved in the scenario planning process?
4 Where does the input come from about potential scenarios the company might encounter?
5 What do you do with the information when you have it?
6 Do you use potential scenarios as one of the bases for your strategy development?

02

Developing an Appropriate Strategy

How to develop a strategy that makes sense for your potential future

Knowing what the company might encounter is one thing; having a plan to deal with those potential scenarios is another. However, there is serious evidence that most strategies miss their targets. According to a study done by Ernst & Young, 66 per cent of corporate strategies are not implemented, and whilst there could be many reasons for this, the main reason is that some strategies have less value than the paper they are printed on.

Most strategies today just don't work.

Too often, strategies are not much more than cleverly worded public relations documents that are filled with vague statements about what the company hopes to accomplish. And, in many cases, these 'strategies' only look at the tip of the iceberg and don't get into the real meat of what the strategy is, or needs to be. If that isn't bad enough, many strategies that I have seen are missing the one extremely critical thing that all of them should have. And that missing element is common sense.

Strategies need not be simple, easy to achieve methods of getting successfully to an organisational future. In fact, they probably should reflect a serious stretch for the organisation. But they do need to also reflect common sense. Common sense in where the company wants to go; common sense in how it will get there; and common sense in what it will take to do so. And because a company strategy is something that everyone in the company needs to understand, it should be explained in plain talk. Strategies are meant to be understood; otherwise, it would be difficult for employees to know what to do, when to do it, and for what reasons. The strategy should not look like a pile of glossy mumbo-jumbo that only some city analyst can understand (or at least say he understands). It should be clear and concise; it should be laced with common sense; and it should paint a picture that everyone in the company can understand.

Additionally, a good strategy is one that incentivises employees to become committed to it. This is one of those common sense things – if there is no reason that employees should buy into implementing the strategy, they won't. Employees, in most cases, will tell you that they have enough to do in their day-to-day jobs; and being involved in the implementation of a strategy means doing extra work. For employees to be willing to buy-in to doing that extra work, they need to realise that there is something in it for them. Incentives don't mean you have to pay them more; incentivising employees means that they have to know that their work (and their additional work) is valued and appreciated.

> Without alignment, understanding and incentives, you will
> not get commitment.

Many strategies are littered with goals, targets and activities that
can be overwhelming. And, in most cases, are not even supportive
of the vision of the company. When employees see this, they
sense that all the additional activity that they will be asked to do
will be fruitless, and that mental model is not conducive for
building commitment around a strategy.

A good strategy has common sense laced throughout it; it
needs to be developed with input from various parts of the
organisation; it should incentivise employees to become
committed to it; and it must be doable. If any of these elements is
lacking, the next time that someone does a study to see how
many strategies actually work, the number of failed ones will
undoubtedly go over 66 per cent.

The failure rates on strategies in organisations is a frightful
indictment of the ability of management to make the right
decisions, at the right times, for the right reasons. And it doesn't
need to be like this.

There are many clever strategy methods available to follow (just
go to Google and type in 'strategic planning'), but I tend to lean
to something that I first became aware of years ago.

The Japanese had for some time been working to improve the
quality of the products that they produced and, to help them do
this, a set of tools was developed that, over time, became known as
the Seven Quality Control tools. You probably use some of them
right now. They include such things as Pareto Charts, Check
Sheets, Control Charts, Scatter Diagrams, Cause and Effect
Diagrams and Histograms. But it didn't take the Japanese
manufacturers long to realise that, whilst they were now able to
ensure that quality products were coming out of their factories,
quite often they were still not making the right decisions about
what to make, what direction to go and what strategy to use to get

there. And because of this, a new set of tools was developed. These tools – the Seven Management and Planning Tools (7M&P) – filled the gap of what strategic planning had been missing for so long. The 7M&P tools took all the ambiguity out of the decision-making process. I will say this again – *the 7M&P tools take the ambiguity out of the decision-making process*. They do not replace the decision-making process; they only take the *ambiguity* out of what to do, when to do it, and for what reasons. They are the vehicles that put common sense back into strategic planning.

There are several key elements of the strategy that need to be clear before building the roadmap. First, it is extremely important to have a clear picture of what you want the organisation to look like in the future. This picture, the organisational vision, needs to look not only at the typically recognisable features of that future like the organisational size, level of revenues and profits, market share and scope of business; it also needs to make clear the elements that can enable these things to occur. These organisational drivers include such elements as organisational culture, the strength of the ability to deliver profits, the levels of alignment and commitment to organisational goals, the impact of competitive threats, and the capacity of management to make effective decisions. Without exploring some of these elements, the chances of your organisation being able to achieve its vision are indeed slim.

> **If the people can't see where they need to go, they will never get there.**

Just knowing what these elements are is only good if you have a way to put them together in a sound plan that the entire organisation can use to get to where you want it to go; and my belief has always been that this is a good place to use some planning tools.

I am keenly aware of all the strategic planning processes and tools that are out there. But one of the things that disturbs me about them is that they seem to have been developed for specific situations, and if that is not problematic enough, many of them seem to have been developed in order to sell books – strange you might think for an author to say, but every time a 'new' way appears, we read about it in the latest business book. I do believe in planning tools and processes, but I tend to look at the issue a bit differently. I think that a good planning process is one that has been proven to work in *any* organisational sector, and has done so for more than a few years. A good planning process is one that uses common sense to help an organisation both understand where it currently is, but also how it can get to where it wants to go. And that is exactly what I am going to show you.

These tools have been in use for over 20 years and I have used them repeatedly with great success. They were selected due to their ability to help resolve several key issues that managers continually seem to get stuck on: exactly what to do, what happens when it is done, and how to measure it. The tools or, more appropriately, toolboxes, are Hoshin Planning, Systems Thinking, and pieces of the Balanced Scorecard (of which there has been much written previously).

Hoshin Planning or, as some know it, Policy Deployment, is a way in which to sort out the myriad possibilities of actions for an organisation to do to realise its potential into the vital few actions that will create the highest leverage for improving their performance. The real key of Hoshin Planning is the way in which the prioritised actions – these are the vital few things that will really make a difference – are cascaded down throughout a department, a division or even an entire company. This ensures that everyone is doing what needs to be done, when it needs to be done. Systems thinking acts like a toolbox that helps managers understand the implications of initiatives on the current and future company situation. This is crucial to avoid the unintended consequences that quite often accompany initiatives that a company tries to deploy. A Balanced Scorecard is method that can be used to effectively measure the results of company initiatives.

Before I get into how to use the tools effectively, it might be useful to list a series of 'rules' that apply to strategy development.

1 Strategies should be fixed and not change – unless there is a good reason to do so.
2 Strategies should reflect the path between the organisational vision (where the company wants to go) and where it is now (the company's current reality).
3 An organisational vision should not change – unless, like rule number 1, there is a good reason to do so.
4 Strategies should reflect and identify contingencies that the company may have to follow in case something unforeseen occurs (but with solid scenario work *before* the strategy is developed, this need will most probably be diminished).
5 Strategies, and the goals and targets that come out of them, need to be measurable, accountable and have specific timelines that are rational and common sense.
6 Strategies need to be shared with and understood by all the employees.
7 Strategies should be developed with the assistance and input of a diagonally cut cross-section of the company (this would include front-line employees – the ones who really know how to get things done) and union members. If the company's management is smart, the development of their strategy will be done with the help of suppliers and customers.
8 Strategies should not be a product of reactive thinking but, instead, a proactive approach to ensuring the company can realise its potential.
9 Strategies have to be 'doable'. They should reflect employee and managerial stretch, but they must be able to be followed. This means that they need to take into consideration what the employees and managers are actually capable of accomplishing. If they currently aren't able to accomplish what the strategy is, then the plan needs to take that into consideration and

provide for training and development for them (which it should probably include anyway).

10 A strategy needs to take into consideration that the managers and employees of the company have their current 'day jobs' to do as well, and the strategy should not be at odds with what those are but, instead, leverage those to help the company realise its potential.

11 A sound strategy is a blending of hard data and the beliefs and assumptions of those who will have to implement it. The data is needed to ensure that the strategic path is not going down a road that does not represent common sense; and the beliefs and assumptions are needed when working out the best ways to ensure that the strategy will be successful.

The whole issue around rule 11 – hard data v. beliefs and assumptions – is something that anyone responsible for the development of a strategy needs to consider. I am a firm believer that decisions that are made without data behind them are akin to driving a car at high speed whilst blindfolded. However, I am also quite aware of the fact that no amount of data can overcome the beliefs and assumptions people have about the best way to do something. And because of this, strategy development needs to be done with both. Be sure to use data when trying to understand the current competitive environment your organisation is in and how your organisational performance can be used effectively in the future through financial aspects. But all the data in the world will not be able to tell you how the employees, suppliers, customers and various other external groups will perceive the strategy, and support or attempt to stall it. For this reason, it is important to be willing to be open to having a cross-sectional group of employees involved in the development of the strategy and its implementation plan. I have seen quite a few plans that have been developed by 'planners' within a company, but with no input from the front-line employees. And when the plan is rolled-out, the front-line workers just smile – they are the people in an organisation who usually *really* know how to get things done and, given the opportunity, are eager to help. Cutting them out of a planning process just because they are 'front-line' employees and not 'planners', is about as rational as running as fast as you can into a brick wall.

The Hunco Group: a myopic view on strategy

Hunco is, on the surface, a story of incredible success. Begun over a decade ago by a man who had a vision about how to build and run a company, Hunco is what most entrepreneurs dream all night about. But as we know, some dreams have a darker side to them, and in the case of Hunco, it has turned out to be a story of missed opportunities because the senior people couldn't make their strategy work over time.

When I first heard about Hunco, I was very impressed. After talking to the CEO, it became clear to me that here was a man whose vision was so incredibly clear – he knew what he wanted to create and what he wanted his company to become – but, unfortunately, his vision was not a complete one. He would regale me with stories about why he started the company; how he was able to make it grow to what it had become; and where he wanted it to go. His ability to communicate the story was incredible, but when it became time to explain several key elements of it, the picture started to become blurry; and his explanation was that these elements of the vision were not that important. If he could keep the company growing, all would be well. Well, that is what he said.

The company had grown and grown relatively consistently since it began. Hunco had begun as a one–person service provider, but because the 'one person' (the current CEO) was so good at what he did, and because he was able to share his vision so vividly, soon it was two people, then three, then five, and soon it was an organisation with more than 20 people employed. And they were making money because they were good at what they did. The CEO had personally hired the additional employees and trained and inspired them to greatness within Hunco. But running a 20-person company is not quite as easy as running a company in which you are the only employee. So, he hired an office manager and went about growing the company more.

A central part of his vision was to become the supplier of choice for the services he provided and as the company grew, it became clearer and clearer to him that he was following the right strategy to do so. And the strategy? Get work, hire competent people to do the work, get more work, hire more people, get more work . . . you probably have the picture by now. When you have a company of that size (up to 20 people) you can get away with a simple strategy; but when a company begins to demonstrate serious growth (by now, Hunco was hiring employees in anticipation of increased growth), the strategic view needs to be more complete and comprehensive.

By the time that Hunco had grown to over 100 people, they had expanded their reach beyond France and were operating in most of continental Europe and the UK. And with this expansion came employees from countries other than France, and with them came cultural baggage. Still, the CEO was able to spread his vision and see continued growth. Very few employees became disenchanted with where the organisation was going – they were all paid extremely well – or with management's push to grow and grow and grow. And when someone 'didn't fit' (the CEO's words) they were simply let go and replaced by someone who did buy into the vision of being part of something great.

After several years of unabated growth, the company suddenly ground to a halt. Yes, they were still relatively profitable, but the ongoing growth pattern had ceased and the CEO was not happy at all. He reorganised the company, put an emphasis onto internal learning, and began paying out bonuses in company stock. And within a short time, the growth pattern resumed once again.

Sales were booming; customers were thrilled with what Hunco was doing for them; and the ever-growing number of employees' wallets were getting thicker and thicker. But after several more years, the growth pattern suddenly stopped again. This was, in the eyes of the CEO, just plain unacceptable. It didn't matter if the economy was good or bad; Hunco had a service to provide that almost every organisation needed, and he was bound and determined to get his strategic growth goals back on track. Once again, the company was reorganised and additional efforts were put into ensuring that the employees were competent enough to sell and deliver the services. And sure as fish goes with chips, the growth pattern returned.

Clearly, this CEO was a smart man. As a matter of fact, he is one of the smartest business leaders I have ever met. But his view on what was occurring was a bit myopic. What he wanted was to realise his vision, and the only way he could do that was to keep the company growing. But as he expanded the company more and more – validation in his mind that the strategy was working – more and more elements that the strategy had overlooked began to surface. The senior leadership team that the CEO had put in place were all sharp guys, and whilst many of them (the senior team, after 10 years of growth, consisted of a dozen people) did buy into the vision, the variation in *how* some of them saw it began to cause problems. The most senior of the senior team (this does sound a bit like something George Orwell wrote), however, were all in a nice line. The strategy was to grow, and that is what the company would do. And if some of the other senior guys (in the company hierarchy, you could be a member of the senior team, but if you weren't an operations person, you were not thought of as part of the 'real team') weren't prepared to follow in a lock-step fashion, they would just be sent away.

When I first met the CEO, the company had a headcount of about 500 people, spread over several continents. When he was telling me his vision, he made it quite clear that his company would, in three or four years, be over double in size, both in headcount and revenue terms. At the time, it appeared that he would be able to realise his vision. But that was before it became apparent that there were elements of the vision that hadn't been considered, much less planned for. One of those 'missed' elements was the mental models of the employees.

Developing a strategy means developing a strategy that encompasses all the elements of what the organisation (or the senior management team, or the Board) wants the organisation to look like in the future. This is far more expansive than just identifying the easy to identify indicators of success, such as revenues and headcounts. One should not underestimate the importance of identifying what the employees' mental models will need to be, and what impact that will have on the organisational culture. In the case of Hunco there were, after a dozen years, enough employees who, on the surface acted out what the senior guys expected from them, but in reality had lost much of the commitment they came in with when they first heard the vision. This was, I was told through many interviews, largely due to what was perceived to be a double standard going on in the home office.

Employees were repeatedly being told of the need to be fiscally responsible, yet it was open knowledge that the senior guys were spending money as if the company was printing it, with major expenses being lost through some poor senior hiring decisions. Policies appeared that were explicitly stated to cover the entire organisation and yet, for some reason, the senior team were able to do what they wanted to do, when they wanted to do it. Performance metrics were put in place that, instead of increasing real performance, simply caused employees to increase their already high skills at gaming the system; and the only people who were caught out were the ones who were considered to be 'marginal' by the senior team. And if all this weren't enough, when it became time to go through one of the several year cycles of reorganisation that the company was experiencing, the 'people first' company handled redundancy decisions as if the employees being shunted out the door were mere commodities.

It has been several years since I first heard about the vision of Hunco, and the CEO's picture of a company that would double everything every three or four years. And at last count, the company is almost exactly where it was several years ago. Quite obviously, something is wrong with their strategy and, sadly, the senior guys don't see it, with their response to the non-sustainable growth pattern being to just get everyone to work harder.

Strategies like the one at Hunco – that don't seem to deliver the desired strategic gains that are hoped for – are clearly missing something. If they were complete and sound, the company would be where the CEO had wanted it to be. In most cases like this, the missing elements are akin to looking at the moon, and only seeing a round, flat disc in the sky. And for many years, this is what people saw, but we know that the moon is a crater-encrusted sphere. Our problem is that due to where the moon is in relation to the earth, we are only able to see one side of it. It takes extraordinary effort to see the entire surface of the moon, from pole to pole, around the entire circumference of it. Through the extraordinary effort that has been expended, we have been able to map out the entire surface of the moon. We know what the surface is like; we even know what it is like to be on the surface of it. But the only way we know all this is because we had made the conscious decision to find out. Developing a strategy that can work over time requires the same type of commitment and effort.

Companies that are serious – and I mean really serious – about realising their potential need to identify all the various elements of their future desired vision. Because if they don't, their companies will be in the same situation that Hunco has found itself – stuck with little manoeuvring room other than to change at the most senior level. And apparently that isn't going to happen, so whilst Hunco will probably always be out there, doing great work for their customers, the chances that it will be able to realise its potential are slim. What a pity that is.

03

Making the Strategy Work
How to enlist your employees into your strategic vision

Planning and implementation of that planning is thought by many to be something we just don't need to do. Hardly. As Yogi Berra, the famous catcher for the New York Yankee baseball team, is purported to have said, *'when you come to a fork in the road, take it'*. That is the situation in many companies today. Management is invariably at a fork in the road and undoubtedly they will take it. Unfortunately for the employees and customers of those companies, the choice of direction at the fork is made by guesswork at best.

> **Tapping into the imagination of people can ensure the realisation and potential of an organisation.**

Nancy Austin, co-author of *Passion for Excellence*, at a recent presentation in the United States, stated, *'the first principle of management is that the driving force for the developments of new products is not technology, not money, but the imagination of people*'. The statement not only holds true for the development of new products, but the way in which organisations deal with the increasing demands of customers, both internal and external. There are organisations that have invested in the latest technology. There are organisations that seem to have bottomless pockets of money. However, there is not a single organisation that can possibly expect to survive into the next decade without people who can innovate. It is these people, with the collective ability to be effective, that will create the future for organisations. One question that might be on our minds is, '*do they have the skills to do this?*'

In her book *Whole Earth Models and Systems*, Donella Meadows states, '*we think that because we understand one, we should be able to understand two, because one and one make two*'. Of course, because we understand the concept of one does not simply mean that we will understand the concept of two. To do this, we need to focus on the word *and*. 'And' is a word that has implications that reach far beyond mathematics. 'And' is a word that begins to allude to the capacity to take knowledge and shift that knowledge into doing – implementing that knowledge. It is the '*and*' that sets us thinking of not only what we do with that knowledge, but how to use it to the best advantage.

If there was one way in which to summarise this planning and deployment process, it would be that the processes act a bit like a funnel. When the employees of a company are faced with the need to become more effective, they have two ways they can go. They can either try to do everything better or begin to prioritise how they spend their time doing whatever they do so they can focus on improving those few, vital, critical things than provide the highest leverage toward becoming effective. I believe that the second option is the best – sorting out all the 'stuff' employees do into the few, vital, critical things that will increase their effectiveness.

Before employees can work to become more effective in improving performance, they must know where the company is going. So, beginning at the beginning, some words about vision.

Vision

Knowing what to do is a function of leadership on all levels. My belief has always been that an effective leader is one who creates an environment in which all the employees of an organisation can become effective, i.e. knowing what to do. This means that the senior management team or CEO are not the only people or group responsible for the development of an organisational vision. This is, of course, only applicable if the company is really serious about getting better.

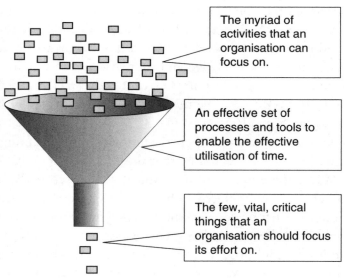

The myriad of activities that an organisation can focus on.

An effective set of processes and tools to enable the effective utilisation of time.

The few, vital, critical things that an organisation should focus its effort on.

Figure 6

In many cases, the vision of an organisation is not clear. Oh, I know the words of the vision statement are usually concise, but the clarity of a vision is a function of the people who need to 'see' that picture. They need to be able to understand not only what the vision statement says, but also what it means to them and to those they work with. If the employees of a company are supposed to be responsible for building an automobile that attained exceptional mileage, a crucial element for their success would be the people who are designing the engine knowing the parameters of the rest of the car. The parameters are the size and weight of the car, the capacity of fuel, the aerodynamics of the body – all the other stuff that makes up a car. The exterior design will have a high impact on the mileage; the chassis design will have a high impact on the mileage – if all the people responsible for their parts of the car (the piece of the vision) are not able to see the other 'visions', there is little chance that they will be able to make a car that makes any sense at all. In short, there will be no chance in hell that the car will work well, which means no chance in hell that anyone will buy it. Vision, and the ability to see that vision, is a key to organisational alignment, and alignment is a key element in enabling the realisation of organisational potential.

Indicators of movement toward a vision

After a vision is developed, it is important to be able to determine what indicators will signal that the people are actually making progress in moving toward it. The indicators are the signposts that you see along the journey, and will be critical when you begin to convert what you learn into something you can do differently. Without indicators of progress toward a vision, it will be impossible to measure the progress you are making.

The indicators are developed through a process known as the Affinity Process, or KJ (from its Japanese origins), in several stages. In using the KJ to develop indicators of vision attainment, a group of people that have been assembled from multiple areas of the company sit down and identify all the indicators they can. In step 1, these 'outputs' are written onto self-sticking notes in a format of three to six words, and should include a verb. The verb is very important as movement toward a vision requires action and, consequently, an action word can be very helpful to ensure that there is clarity on what the brainstormed indicator really means.

Figure 7 Affinity Process, Step 1 – brainstormed outputs

Once the people have identified as many indicators as they can, the outputs are sorted into themes in step 2. These themes are groups of indicators that have some affinity to each other. An example might be, if we were to brainstorm all the foods we could think of, and then sort them into themes that had some affinity to each other, we might end up with meats, fish, fruits, vegetables, etc. An important part of the sorting operation is the rules associated with it.

Rule 1 First, do not try to begin the process with titles for the themes already in your head – the themes will become clear as the process moves forward.

Rule 2 Make sure that in the sorting process, each person who is working on it feels free to group outputs as he or she sees fit. Don't try to convince anyone that an output should end up with any other output.

Rule 3 Don't allow talking during this process. This process is supposed to be highly visual and talking may run the risk of someone trying to convince someone else of where to put an output. And as you can imagine, they will try to disregard this rule and talk. Get tough and tell them no talking, period.

Rule 4 Don't let the sorting process go on too long. If the sorting process drags on, one of two things will happen – either the outputs being sorted will end up in one very large theme group, or they will end up in as many groups as there are outputs. Either one is bad, so when the sorting process begins to slow down – when the group look like they are struggling to figure out which outputs go where – then cut it off.

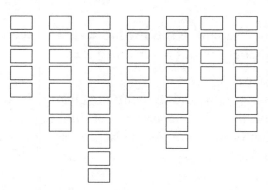

Figure 8 Affinity Process, Step 2 – sorted outputs

In step 3, theme titles are developed. These titles, or header cards, are a way to capture the thoughts that went into the brainstorming process. The development of the headers is done by getting a facilitator – the facilitator could be you, but it is better if it is someone who is not connected to the purpose of the planning – to read all the outputs in any one column and then asking the group what the message is that the outputs are telling, i.e. what is the theme in the column. If there are any outputs that seem to address something other than the prevalent theme, simply remove them for later use. Once the theme title is selected, write that title on a header card and put it at the top of the column.

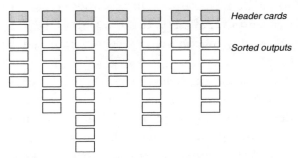

Figure 9 Affinity Process Step 3 – developing theme titles

AFFINITY PROCESS – REVIEW

Purpose

The Affinity Diagram (KJ) is used to sort out a number of themes from a group of brainstormed ideas.

When to use

When facts, opinions and thoughts are chaotic, or when a breakthrough in traditional patterns of thinking is needed. When a team or group of people lacks unity or consensus in their thinking.

Process

- State the issue: in this example, 'what are the indicators that we will see to demonstrate we are moving toward our vision'. Ensure that the entire team or group fully understands the question under consideration.
- Brainstorm ideas to resolve a problem or issue.
- Record the brainstormed ideas on 3 × 5 self-sticking notes.
- All brainstormed ideas should be in the format of three to six words, and should contain a verb.
- Place the ideas on a whiteboard in random placement (Step 1).

There are several things that are important to remember in the development of the header cards.

1 The header card is a reflection of the theme that is present in a column. That is to say, the header card represents the theme that is there, but does not necessarily represent all the potential ideas within that theme.
2 The header cards should, just as the initial brainstormed outputs, contain three to six words, including a verb – these header cards represent actions, and should always have an action word within them.

● After brainstorming is completed, begin to sort the ideas into themes that have an affinity to each other (Step 2).
● Sorting should be completed without talking or motioning as to which ideas belong with others.
● Develop 'header cards' that reflect the general theme that is evident from the ideas (Step 3).
● Review completed diagram to make sure it reflects common sense.

Guidelines for facilitation

● Remind the team to follow the guidelines for effective brainstorming.
● Stick with the rule of three to six words per note, with a verb.
● Reaffirm the silence guideline for the sorting process. Allow talking only on two situations – to clarify the meaning of an idea or to request a duplicate.
● Ensure that each vertical column reflects only one theme.
● Ensure that the header cards truly reflect the essence of the theme below.

3 Do not try to force outputs into certain themes. This process is a natural one, and if you end up with several outputs that do not seem to have 'homes' in the existing themes, then they most probably represent another theme(s). Even a one–output theme should have a header card, even if it says the same thing as the card itself.

When the Affinity Process is completed, you will have something that looks like Figure 9. There is no fixed rule as to how many columns you will end up with, regardless of how many outputs you begin with. This happens through natural selection – it just sorts itself out based on how you view a specific situation. Let the sorting process take care of itself. As this process was done to determine how the company (or the department or division or whatever) would be able to know if it was making progress moving toward its vision, the thing to look for – the central indicators – are the header cards. Without the header cards – the themes associated with movement toward a collective vision – the process of looking for indicators of movement would be too unwieldy. The header cards synthesise what to look for into a small group of key indicators.

Determination of Driving Indicators

Once the indicators of positive movement toward a vision have been determined, it is important to be able to identify which of those indicators are the most critical to watch for. Here is the analogy: you are in a car driving from London to Barcelona, Spain. Some of the indicators of progress might be a) the temperature increases the closer you are to Barcelona, b) you see the sun more and more during the day as you get closer to Barcelona, c) the people you talk to on this journey speak different languages as you go further and further south, and d) the distance to Barcelona on road signs get smaller and smaller as you get closer to your destination. Now, think about it. Indicator A is okay, but sometimes the temperature can be erratic so that may not be the best indicator to follow; indicator B might be influenced by weather patterns that are random at best, so that may not be the best indicator; indicator C is sort of relative, as there are people who live in Edinburgh that some Londoners don't understand. Therefore, it makes common sense that indicator D is the most important one to watch for. Right? Okay, so how can you find the indicator of movement toward your vision?

This can be done through another tool of the Hoshin toolbox known as the Interrelationship Digraph (ID), which can look quite complex at first glance, but helps to take the ambiguity out of the decision process regarding what vision indicator is most critical, i.e. which one to watch for.

The first step in using this tool is to duplicate all of the headers that were developed in the Affinity Process. Note: do not just use the Affinity headers, but duplicate them, because it's really important to keep the outputs from each tool to document all the steps that took place in developing the plan. The duplicate header cards should be placed on a flip chart or brown paper in a circular pattern. The pattern will look more circular with more headers than with less, but use only the headers that were developed in the KJ.

The facilitator who is helping with the process then begins to ask the assembled group which of these headers has a driving or influential relationship with the others. The word 'driving' may mean different things to different people, but the best way to describe it is, a driver is something that causes something else to happen. Okay? This process of determining driving relationships is asked of one relationship at a time. I have found that it is best to begin at the 12 o'clock position and ask if that header card has a driving relationship with the next header card that is located clockwise from the top. Remember, the real question is, 'if we do this (one of the header cards), will it cause this (the other header card) to happen? How about the other direction? If we do the other header card, will it cause the first one to happen? Now, if the people think that there is a driving relationship, the facilitator would draw an arrow from the driver to the one that is driven. If there is no driving relationship, then no line is drawn.

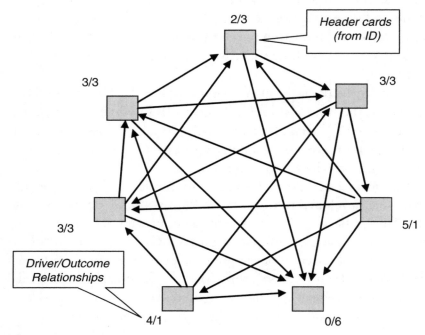

Figure 10 The Interrelationship Digraph

When using the ID to determine 'priority of importance', it is crucial to remember that all the header cards are related – they all represent themes that came from the same question in the Affinity Process. However, all the header cards do not necessarily have driving (causal) relationships with each other. After the first relationship is determined, the facilitator should go on to the next potential relationship (the header card located at 12 o'clock and the second card located clockwise from the top). This process continues until all of the header cards are checked for driving relationships to the one at the top. Then the facilitator begins with the first card located clockwise from the top and repeats the entire process. After determining all of those relationships, the facilitator moves on to the next card, until every potential relationship has been evaluated. This may sound sort of complicated, but after you use the tool a couple of times, it is quite easy. The only trick is asking the question right, so go back a page or so and read how to do this again.

Several key points when using the ID include, 1) there can only be one arrow between any two header cards (there is no such thing as a relationship that 'drives' both ways, and 2) if the group is at an impasse regarding the driving direction between any two header cards, the facilitator should draw a dotted line between those two cards; tell you why in a minute. At the end of the process of determining driving relationships, the number of relationships is counted and indicated on the chart. If a header card has two arrows going out of it, and three arrows going into it, the indication would be noted as 2/3. This means that that header card (or more importantly, the message that is contained in the theme) drives two other themes, but it is an outcome of three other themes. If the number is 5/1, it would mean that the header card (theme) actually drives and influences five other themes, and is only an outcome of one. This would indicate a high driving influence and would then be considered something to look for, as opposed to an outcome. Remember what I said about using a dotted line when you can't get agreement on the driving direction? After you count up all the relationships, then you can go back and look at the dotted lines. If a relationship that has a dotted line may change the overall answer, then it might be worth trying to resolve the impasse. If resolving the dotted line impasse won't make any difference in the overall answer, don't waste your time.

The completed ID can look rather chaotic, with lines and arrowheads everywhere (based on the number of header cards used). The clarity comes from understanding what the group is looking for – which header card (theme) drives and influences the most other themes. It is that theme that will be the most critical to look for when determining progress in movement toward a vision. One of the central reasons to use the ID is that it is almost impossible to watch for all the indicators of movement toward a vision, and as the KJ begins to sort that myriad of indicators down to a manageable few, the ID helps us to understand which of those few are the most important to watch for.

Okay, now to try to make this all a bit clearer, I am going to show you a real ID that was done with a client several years ago. As you can imagine, I have had to 'clean it up' a bit to remove any names that might cause the client concern. Now as you look at the picture, you need to keep several things in mind. First of all, this example is quite a rarity — in most cases, IDs only have

---

INTERRELATIONSHIP DIGRAPH – REVIEW

Purpose
The Interrelationship Digraph (ID) is used to graphically map out the cause and effect links among all items under consideration, and to identify the most fundamental drivers and outcomes among all the related items.

When to use
When a large number of interrelated issues need to be better defined and the driving relationships between them determined.

Process

- Display the related issues on self-sticking notes in a circular pattern on a flip chart.
- Determine the relationships between them and draw arrows designating the relationship direction. Begin with any note and ask the question, 'does this item have a driving relationship with the next note, and if it does, which way does it go?' Repeat the question for each note around the circular pattern. Then begin again with the next note.

---

about six to nine headers floating around. This one has 15, chiefly because the organisation was really complex and they had a lot of issues to sort out. Second, as you look at the picture, think of which of these headers you would have thought to be the big driver. In the real organisation that this came from, everyone (well, almost everyone – 18 of the 20 people in the planning group) was convinced that the big driver would come out to be Improve Organisational Climate. This was because they all were so convinced that if they just get that right, everything else would fall into place. Guess what? The ID quite often results in the illumination of real counter-intuitive thinking. Third, don't get caught up in the apparent chaos of all the arrows running about.

- Ask the question only once for each potential relationship, drawing only one arrow between **any** two notes.
- If it is determined that there is no driving relationship between two notes, do not draw any line.
- In the case of a driving relationship in which there is no consensus as to the direction, draw a dotted line with no arrowhead on either end.
- Count up the number of arrows out and arrows in for each note and write that number next to each note: i.e. 4/2 (four arrows out and two arrows in).
- Check to see if the overall answer makes common sense.

Guidelines for facilitation

- Consider the relationship between only two notes at a time.
- Always focus on the question, 'does this item drive that item?'
- Keep the process flowing. Do not let one person dominate the process.
- Do not allow two-way arrows.

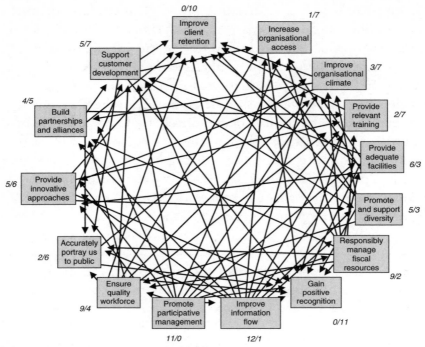

Figure 11 An original Interrelationship Digraph

To get the counts right, all you need to do is look for arrowheads and arrow tails – the rest of the arrow lines are just a bunch of spaghetti. Don't worry about them – count the arrowheads and arrow tails to figure out what is driving what. Okay, take a look.

Okay, breathing again? See, if you just focus on what is important (in the case of an ID, what is important is the number of arrows that are going out of a header card), you can easily figure out which header is the big driver. And believe me, if you are putting efforts to improve performance into a header card that is not the big driver, you will not get the outcomes you want, or the outcomes you need. Your choice.

Development of a Baseline

The next logical step in a planning process to track effectiveness is to determine two things: how much progress has been made in movement toward a vision, and how much effort is currently being expended to accomplish this goal. For these measurements, we use a tool commonly known as an Arachnid Chart.

Arachnid chart

This tool gets its name because it looks like a spider's web. Once again, the process begins with the header cards from the KJ that articulated the various themes revolving around indicators that

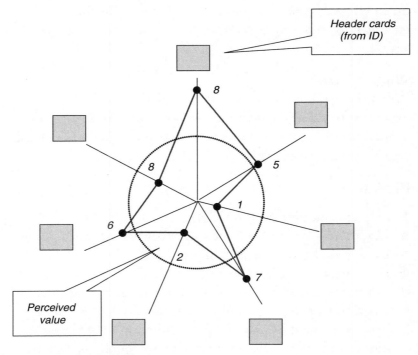

Figure 12 The Arachnid Chart

will show movement toward a vision. The reason to use the same header cards is to make sure that there is some continuity for the overall process, as well as to help to build alignment regarding what indicators are important. The headers are oriented in the same circular pattern as in the Interrelationship Digraph, but with the addition of lines being drawn from the centre of the 'circle' to each header card. The lines look like radius lines of the hypothetical circle and each line represents a rating scale, with a potential range from 0 to 100 (the centre of the circle would be 0, the outside end of each line at a header card would be 100).

ARACHNID CHART – REVIEW

Purpose
The Arachnid Chart (AR) is used to identify either how much effort is currently being expended in achieving a goal or how much progress has been attained in achieving a goal.

When to use
When there is confusion as to how much effort is being expended to achieve a goal, or when baseline information is needed to show potential progress. When consensus is needed regarding current efforts.

Process
- Duplicate header cards from KJ.
- Orient new theme cards into a circular formation.
- Draw radii lines to each theme card.
- Determine which card to begin with.
- Ask the participants to review the theme cards and formulate a belief as to either how much effort is currently being expended by the group/organisation to achieve the goals listed on the theme cards, or how much progress has

The actual ratings are done in percentages and can represent either the amount of progress being made in each theme in movement toward the vision, or the amount of effort currently being expended to accomplish that movement.

The concept of rating current efforts can be difficult for some groups of people, because the rating is based on the perceptions of the group. However, this system works quite well, mainly because it is the perceptions of the group that represent the perceptions of the organisation as a whole. Perceptions, or mental models, drive the behaviours of employees, so to be able to

---

been attained to date in achieving the goal listed on the theme card.

- Ask the participants to identify their perception regarding their perception of the question. Responses should be in the form of 'per cent' of effort or completion.
- Average the participants' responses and determine the average response.
- Plot the average response on the appropriate line of the chart. Note, the centre of the chart equates to 0 per cent, the farthest extremity equates to 100 per cent.
- Continue the process around the chart.
- Connect the plotted percentages with a line.
- Review for sensibility.

Guidelines for facilitation:

- Focus on only one radii line at a time.
- Use common sense when balancing the need for thorough discussion with total risk.
- The amount of effort should never reflect either 0 per cent or 100 per cent.
- If the Arachnid Chart is being used in conjunction with an Interrelationship Digraph, ensure that the circular layout is the same.

determine where an organisation currently is will give an indication of what needs to be done to shift efforts.

The process for using this tool begins with the facilitator asking the following question for each of the header cards, 'how much progress has been made by our organisation in seeing this indicator?' Each person in the process is given the opportunity to 'rate' how much progress has been made and the responses are added up and then divided by the number of people in the group. This gives an average or collective view of how much progress has been made. The average is plotted on the appropriate radii line with a big dot, and then it helps to actually write down the number next to the dot. Don't worry about getting the dot exactly in the right spot. What I mean is, if the number average is 58, putting the dot in about the middle of the radius line is good enough. This is not an exercise to see who is the most anal about being exact – it is an exercise to figure out if there is more progress being made in one area or another. When all the radii lines have been plotted, it is possible to 'connect the dots', giving a graphical representation of the progress being made on all aspects of movement toward the vision.

To determine how much effort is currently being expended to move toward the vision, the same process is followed, with the only change being the question asked. One of the things that happens when the process is completed is that the 'shape' that is an outcome of the process rarely looks circular. This is because equal progress is rarely being made on movement toward the indicators of vision attainment. The same holds true for effort – rarely do we spend equal effort on many things and then expect to get them done. When completed, the two charts can be compared with each other, and with the information supplied through the use of the Interrelationship Digraph. Key things to look for include; is the effort being expended matched up with where the leverage is? Is the effort being expended yielding the results that are being seen? Is the progress that has been made matching up with the key leverage areas?

One caution in using the Arachnid Chart is that the two alternatives – progress seen and efforts being expended – should not be done consecutively. A time gap of several hours should be built into this process. This will help to ensure that the people in the process don't confuse the two questions and, consequently, skew their responses.

Planning What Needs to be Done

This is where most strategies are believed to be. But the reality is that this step just reflects what actions the strategy calls for. Planning on what the organisation will do to achieve its goals can be done in several ways, based on how complex the issues and the way people get work done are. One method to use involves using the Affinity Process once again. This method is quite clean and can provide very clear documentation on why an organisation is doing what it is doing. If this is the process used, the KJ should once again be followed by an Interrelationship Digraph (ID) to act as a screen to focus the efforts on high leverage activities. Once the specific activities are selected through a process, the next step would be to identify the various levels of those activities. For this, it is appropriate to use a Tree Diagram (see Figure 14).

Goal	Targets	Responsibility	Measures	Vehicles	Timeline	Flag
	Determine XYZ corp issues at all levels	See attached relationship document	Issues identified	Issue report	01/12	
Develop value proposition for 'client'	Conduct scans	Dereck White	Scan results compiled	Scan report	01/12	
	Develop targets for meetings	Nick Wilson	Target list compiled	Client list	01/11	■
	Prepare value proposition documentation	Dereck White	Document ready to share with client	Document	01/12	

Figure 13 A Tree Diagram

The Tree Diagram is a tool that is used to 'flesh out' the various activities that the organisation will employ to achieve its goals. This is true on the overall organisational level and on local levels the process is still the same. A Tree Diagram consists of several components: the goal (what is being focused on), targets (activities that are employed to achieve the goal), responsibilities (whomever will be held responsible for the successful completion of the targets), measures (visible ways to know that the targets have been met), vehicles (the tangible, physical evidence that you achieved the goal), timelines (the date by which a target will have been met), and flag (a little box to show the relative status of the target effort, i.e. ¼ filled in = ¼ completed). Sound a little complex? It isn't at all. Just read on.

Typically, for very complex issues, another level can be utilised in a Tree Diagram. That additional level is called the Means. Each target might have one or more Means (an activity that would be completed to make sure that the target gets done). If this were the case, then the responsibilities, measures, vehicles, timelines and flags would accompany each Means.

Here is an example from a piece of work our company did recently. Now don't get distressed about this picture. Let me explain what all the different boxes mean. It basically follows the previous example, with a few exceptions. The main exception is the level of detail that it shows.

The boxes on the left are for the overall goal of the work and the objective of the work. In this case, the goal spoke about implementing a huge supply chain project – this was a big project that would make a major impact on the global company. The objective of the project was to save the company over $20,000,000 within one year. The first column of four boxes was for targets – targets are a bit like level one activities that the company would do to achieve the goal. Note: level one activities are very high level, but extremely important. The next column articulated the various means that would be used to achieve the targets. The third column of boxes is for more detailed means.

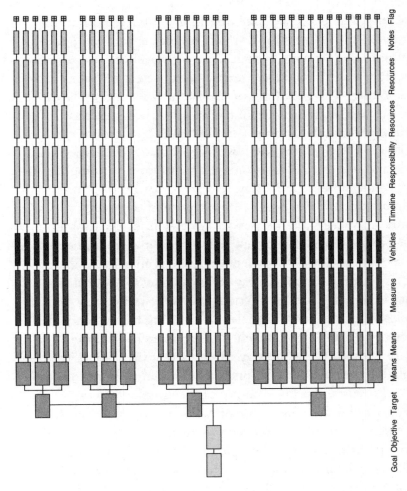

Goal Objective Target Means Means Measures Vehicles Timeline Responsibility Resources Resources Notes Flag

Figure 14 A completed Tree Diagram

Confused? Here is how it works. Whenever a company decides to implement some initiative, it must consider what high level, medium level and detail level activities it will need to perform to achieve the goal, whatever it is. An example – not a business one but one that is pretty generic and personal – of a goal might be to get healthy. The objective might be to live longer and healthier. With me so far? Targets for this goal might be: lose weight, eat better and improve your lifestyle. The first level of means for the lose weight target could be: exercise, improve eating habits and stop smoking. The next level of means for the exercise means might be: have a physical examination to see what exercise programme might be appropriate, find an exercise trainer and join a health facility. See how the flow of goal to targets, targets to means, and means to means shifts the focus from very high level to more and more detail? Okay, let's go back to the picture.

The next column of boxes is for 'measures of success'. Measures of success are the way that you will see that the most detailed level of means is completed. This is important, because my experience shows that whenever there is an activity, there needs to be a really explicit way to know how to see that the activity is completed. The next column is for something we call 'vehicles' or exit criteria. Vehicles are the tangible evidence that the activity has been completed. This is different than the measure – a measure is the way to know that the activity has been completed; the vehicle is the proof of that completion. In most cases, vehicles are reports, minutes of meetings, affidavits, brochures and other tangible documents. I have even seen some cases where vehicles are photos or videotapes – whatever it takes to show that the activity is completed. The whole issue of vehicles is really important, for without the proof you may run the risk that somebody will say that they have completed the activity without any way to check it out. Use the vehicle; the value of it is the key to accountability.

The first of the next six columns is for timeline. The timeline represents the date that the activity will be completed. Not started, not almost done, but totally completed. Determining the appropriate timeline dates requires you to take a look at the critical path of activities. In many cases, activities may take more or less time than you would like, so make sure that you know what is realistic before you start slamming dates onto the tree diagram. The next column is for responsibility. This column is used to identify who will be held responsible for getting the work done on time. Now be careful with this column. The person responsible may or may not be the person who will be doing the actual work. It is just the person who will make sure that whomever is working on the activity gets it done on time. The next two columns are for identifying the resources needed to get the activity done on time. The first of these two is for people resources. This is where you identify who will actually be doing the work – in most cases, it comes out to be a project team or task force members. Once again, be careful here, as you don't want to overload people with project work unless you can cut them some slack on their 'day jobs'. The second of the two resource columns is for other resources that will be applied. This might include financial resources, technology resources or any other additional resources you may need to provide to get the activity done on time.

The second to last column shown is for 'notes'. This is where you can write down anything that you feel is important to keep track of. In many cases, this is where we see things like identification of similar activities or identification of activities that need to be done to ensure that this activity *can be* done. The last column is something we call flag. A flag is simply a square box divided into four quarters. As the work progresses, you fill in one of more of the quadrants of the flag box to show how far along the activity is. You know, when the activity is half done, you fill in half the box. This is especially good to use to keep track of how all the activities (targets, means, means) are doing. It is a lot easier than going over the whole tree diagram all the time.

Now, a logical thing for you to ask is, 'is all this detail really important?' You better believe it is. If you don't go into this type

TREE DIAGRAM – REVIEW

Purpose
The Tree Diagram (TR) is used to map out activities and tasks that are needed to achieve a goal or set of goals. Additionally, the Tree Diagram articulates the measures of attainment, responsibilities, vehicles, timelines and resources needed.

When to use
When assignable tasks must be created. When broad objectives need to be broken down into specific detail.

Process

- Determine goal to be attained.
- Identify actionable steps to attain the goal.
- Identify specific activities that will achieve the steps.
- Identify measures of attainment for each specific activity.

of detail when laying out a big project implementation, I can almost guarantee that you will miss something or mix something up. I have seen it over and over again. Use the tree diagram and put the extra work in up front. The detail will ensure a positive outcome from all your work. Another logical question that I hope you are thinking about is, 'who gets to see the completed tree diagram?' Well, anyone whose name appears on the 'responsibility' column should definitely see it and get a chance to review it. If they believe that the means that they are supposed to get done cannot be done either within the timeline with the resources available or because they are not the appropriate person to get it done, then talk it over and negotiate a solution. Anyone whose name appears as a people resource should also get a chance to see it – they are the ones who will do the additional work, and they will most certainly be concerned about putting time into another project activity and getting their real job done.

- Identify who should be responsible for the attainment of each activity.
- Identify what the tangible evidence would be for each activity attainment.
- Identify when the activity will be completed.
- Identify what resources would be needed to attain the activity.
- Check for sensibility.
- Validate the completed Tree Diagram with those whose names are listed as responsible parties to validate potential for success based on timelines and resources.

Guidelines for facilitation

- Potential levels of detail can be found in an Affinity Diagram.
- Move from general goals (goal) to detail activities (targets).
- At each level of detail, ask, 'What has to happen to accomplish this?'

Determining Relationships

There are several types of relationships that are most often seen when using these tools – relationships between actions and outcomes, relationships between customer's needs and methods that are used to meet those needs, relationships between processes and effectiveness, and relationships between opportunities and potential activities. In all of the ways you can use to determine relationships, the tool that is most commonly used is a Matrix. This is most often used to compare two sets of variables. The only common thing that appears in matrices should be the symbols used to determine the relationships involved.

In the matrix example shown, the two variables being compared are the needs of a client, and the processes that are being used to make sure those needs are actually met. The facilitation process for a matrix is much like other tools. The facilitator, after laying out the matrix, begins by asking which of the variables in the columns has the greatest impact on meeting the need listed in the first horizontal row. The key here is the words, 'greatest impact'. By definition, this means that only one of the variables in the vertical columns can be identified at this point, i.e. there can only be one 'greatest'. When this variable is identified, the facilitator puts a double circle shape in the corresponding matrix cell. The symbols used are really important because it is easier to look at a matrix with symbols and know what is going on, than a matrix where numbers alone are used. The problem with just numbers is that you get caught up in disagreements about the 'absolute value' of a number. Trust me on this – symbols work out a lot better in the long run.

When using matrices, most organisations use the same three symbols to show varying degrees of relationships. The symbols are a double circle, a circle and a triangle. The double circle denotes the strongest possible relationship; the circle denotes a strong relationship; and a triangle denotes a moderately strong relationship. Those are the only three symbols (levels of relationships) that are important to determine. (The story is that the matrix was first used in Japanese industry. The users tried to figure out what kind of symbols would be easily recognised by the workers using the matrices, so they used something that they thought was understood by lots of people. The symbols I have shown you are the same symbols used in Japanese racing forms to represent Win, Place and Show.) Over the years, I have learnt that only one of each symbol shape should be used on each horizontal row. This is to clearly show the strength of relationships – relationships other than the top three levels are rarely important to focus on and, consequently, their strength is not worth wasting time to figure out.

Now for all you accountant types out there who have noticed that the matrix example didn't get any votes under the column of 'billing', here is why. Yes, of course billing is important in any

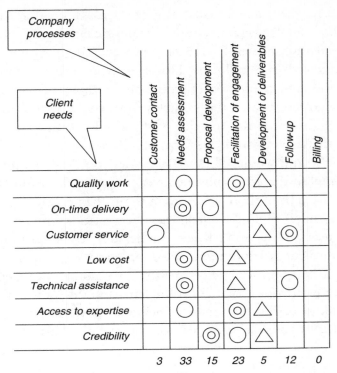

Figure 15 A matrix

business. When this example was developed (a real example from a client), the finance guys went orbital because they said that if the company didn't do any billing, the company wouldn't exist much longer. Right, of course. But the question was, '*which process has the strongest relationship to meeting the needs of the customers?*' Now think about it. How many customers give two hoots if they receive an invoice from you? Not too many. And getting an invoice is not exactly one of the really hot needs of your customers, is it? Yes, billing is important, but it is not as important to your customers as the way in which you meet their needs. Sometimes, using the matrix – and all the other tools – results in an outcome that is really counter intuitive. Trust the process!

Another way to use a matrix is when deploying a strategic plan throughout an organisational population, usually during the implementation phase of a planning process. Once again, the same basic process is followed. However, when using a matrix to deploy the implementation of a plan, the variables would be different. In most cases, the variables used would be the overall organisational initiatives (on the left-hand side of the matrix), and what activities you would perform on the top of the matrix (see Figure 17). You would fill in the activities you think appropriate to accomplish the goals and initiatives, and then determine the relative strength of those activities in the matrix cells using the matrix symbols of double circle (strongest relationship), circle (strong relationship) and triangle (moderately strong relationship). This information would then be forwarded to your supervisor for review. When approved, another matrix would be put together, this time with your activities on the left-hand side of the matrix and blank spaces on the top. This new matrix would be forwarded to your direct reports for completion. This process of

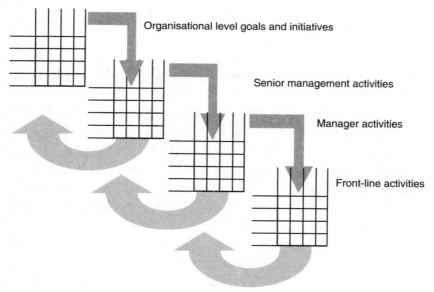

Figure 16 The cascading process of the matrices

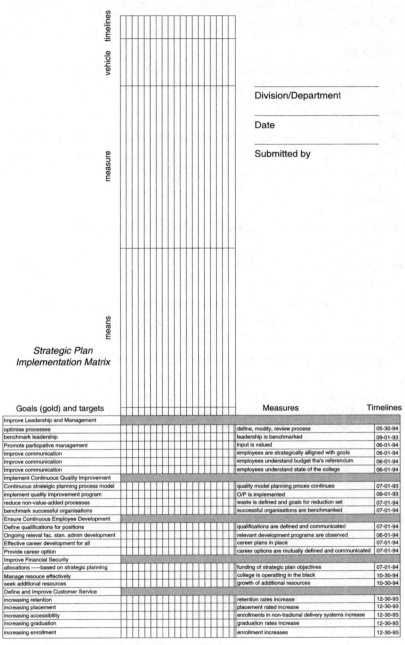

vehicle timelines

measure

means

Division/Department

Date

Submitted by

Strategic Plan
Implementation Matrix

Goals (gold) and targets	Measures	Timelines
Improve Leadership and Management		
optimise processes	define, modity, review process	05-30-94
benchmark leadership	leadership is benchmarked	09-01-93
Promote partipcative management	input is valued	06-01-94
Improve communication	employees are strategically alligned with goals	06-01-94
Improve communication	employees understand budget tha's referendum	06-01-94
Improve communication	employees understand state of the collegs	06-01-94
Implement Continuous Quality Improvement		
Continuous strateigic planning process model	quality model planning proces continues	07-01-93
implement quality improvement program	O/P is implemented	09-01-93
reduce non-value-added processes	waste is defined and goals for reduction set	07-01-94
benchmark successful organisations	successful organisations are benchmanked	07-01-94
Ensure Continuous Employee Development		
Define qualifications for positions	qualifications are defined and communicated	07-01-94
Ongoing reieval fac. stan. admin development	relevant development programs are observed	06-01-94
Effective career development for all	career plans in place	07-01-94
Provide career option	career options are mutually defined and communicated	07-01-94
Improve Financial Security		
allocations -----based on strategic planning	funding of strategic plan objectives	07-01-94
Manage resouce effectively	college is operatting in the black	10-30-94
seek additional resources	growth of additional resources	10-30-94
Define and Improve Customer Service		
increasing retention	retention rates increase	12-30-93
increasing placement	placement rated increase	12-30-93
increasing accessibility	enrollments in non-tradional delivery systems increase	12-30-93
increasing graduation	graduation rates increase	12-30-93
increasing enrollment	enrollment increases	12-30-93

Figure 17 Strategic Plan Implementation Matrix

MATRIX – REVIEW

Purpose
A Matrix is used to identify the connection of relationships between two or more variables.

When to use
When there is low alignment about the connection between activities and needs of customers; when there is low alignment about which efforts deliver the best results.

Process

- Identify the two sets of variables to compare with each other.
- Determine which of the set of variables you wish to make the comparison with.
- List the variables you wish to compare on the horizontal axis and the comparing variables on the vertical axis.
- Ask participants which of the horizontal variables has the strongest impact on the first of the vertically placed variables (note, by definition, there can only be one 'strongest'). Place a double circle in the cell where the two variables meet.

deeper and deeper levels of an organisation all tracking to the same goals can help to ensure organisational alignment in activities that are targeted at achieving a set of goals and initiatives. It is the cascading process of the matrices, both upwards and downwards, that enables the alignment.

The objective of all this is to ensure that the strategy is based on common sense around reality, and also to ensure that the rationale behind the strategy can be effectively deployed throughout the organisation. The level of difficulty doing this – deploying actions throughout the company – is based on how complex the organisation is and how the work actually gets done. One method

- Ask participants which of the remaining horizontal variables has the next strongest impact and place a circle in the cell where these two variables meet.
- If needed, ask participants which of the remaining variables has the third strongest relationship and place a triangle in the cell where the two variables meet.
- Ask the participants which of the horizontal variables has the strongest impact on the second of the vertically placed variables and continue as before.
- Follow this process until all the vertically placed variables have been checked.
- Examine which of the horizontally placed variables has the greatest number of symbols under it (and, if necessary, using the traditional matrix values, total the number of points).
- Check for common sense.

Guidelines for facilitation

- Focus on only one of the vertically placed variables at a time.
- Use common sense when making the judgements.
- Use traditional matrix symbols and values for determining which variables demonstrate the strongest relationship.

involves using the Affinity Process once again to figure out which activities are most important. This method is quite clean and can provide very clear documentation on why an organisation is doing what it is doing. If this is the process used, the KJ should once again be followed by an Interrelationship Digraph (ID) to act as a way to know what to focus on.

When all the activities that are planned in an organisation are compared, you may find that some of the activities will cause unintended consequences. If you believe that this may happen, it is appropriate to explore the effect on the organisation and its dynamics. This is an appropriate place to use Systems Thinking.

Understanding Unintended Consequences

Planning on what the organisation will do to achieve its goals can be done in several ways. Systems Thinking is a collection of theories, concepts and tools that can be used to make visible the dynamics at play in organisations. The central concept behind Systems Thinking is that, 'there is more going on than meets the eye'. We use systems thinking to make those things visible. One thing to remember when doing systems thinking work: most people associate systems thinking with causal loop diagrams (CLDs) or maps. A causal loop diagram is not the answer; it is only a reflection of the 'thinking' part of systems thinking. The causal loop diagram is a visible demonstration of the dynamics at play in an organisational situation. Causal loop diagrams are very powerful, as they can illuminate where an intervention is appropriate, most often, as it shows both the positive and negative unintended consequences of that intervention.

There are several key things to think about when using systems thinking. They include:

Cause and effect are not closely related in time and space. We all understand cause and effect – if you touch a hot stove, you will get burnt; an immediate impact (effect) of a cause. But when considering organisational decisions, in most cases, the effects are numerous and are usually not visible until after a delay – in many cases, a considerable delay.

The easy way out leads back in. In most organisations, there is a propensity to take immediate action when faced with a problem. This is classic fire fighting – when a fire is present, it is crucial to put the fire out. But unfortunately, in most cases, putting the fire out only deals with the symptom of the fire and not the underlying, fundamental cause of the fire. And consequently, after a delay, the fire comes back once again. By taking the easy way out of a problem, we tend to find ourselves back in the same situation again.

Behaviours will get worse before they get better. Whenever an organisational population is faced with a change in the way that they do business, their ability to continue their level of productivity is diminished. After a 'learning curve', this level can resume, and usually does. However, the depth and breadth of the slump in productivity are controlled by the ability of the population to learn and apply that learning.

There are no right answers. This 'rule' seems to go against any good consulting methodology, but it is the semantics that are critical here. By definition, if there is a 'right' answer to a question, then every other answer must be 'wrong'. That is clearly not the case when talking about organisations and organisational decision making. There are answers to questions that are most certainly better than others; that does not make them 'right'. Being right is a situational dynamic – what is right today may not appear to be right tomorrow.

Structure drives behaviour. Structure includes the explicit (the policy book) and implicit (the way things really get done) policies

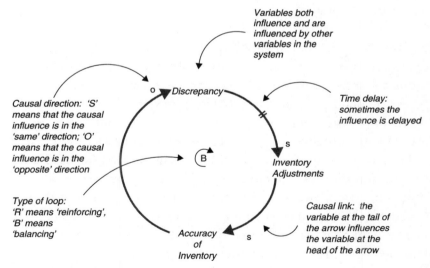

Figure 18 Causal loop diagram

and procedures that cause organisational employees to act in one way or another. Structure also includes the mental models that the employees of an organisation have regarding their beliefs and assumptions of how the organisation should work.

Building causal loop diagrams requires knowledge of several loop elements. These elements are variables, links and directions.

Causal loop diagrams can be extremely helpful when responding to organisational issues. Through the utilisation of systems thinking and causal loop diagrams, you can:

❑ Look for patterns of behaviour . . . 'Has this problem occurred in the past?'
❑ Search for deeper understanding of the problem . . . 'What structures might be causing this behaviour?'
❑ Look for time delays . . . 'What effect will project delays have on our resources?'
❑ Look for unintended consequences . . . 'What would happen if we implemented a specific solution?'

By using systems thinking, and then using causal loop diagrams to make that thinking explicit, it is possible to identify why some problems keep recurring; why certain organisational structures have a tendency to generate problems; what the impact of time delays on a system will be; and what some of the intended and unintended consequences of an implementation process will be.

Here is an example of a causal loop diagram that shows the interrelationships of implementing a knowledge management system in an organisation. The key message here is that, if the system were to be implemented, the potential to learn would increase, thereby increasing the collective level of organisational knowledge – traditionally thought of as good news and an intuitive belief. However, although that dynamic is present, there is another dynamic that is present. As employees learn more, there is the potential that they will apply that learning in different ways, actually fragmenting the long-term potential of the organisation – most definitely an unintended, counter intuitive dynamic. This diagram was instrumental in shifting the mindset of those who were planning the knowledge management implementation in a large, multinational utility.

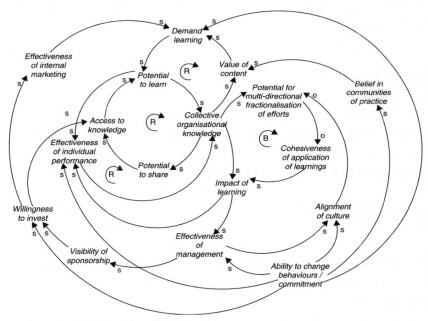

Figure 19 A completed causal loop diagram

When using systems thinking with large-scale organisational implementations, the outcomes can be extremely powerful. Most people would agree that, due to their position in an organisation, they may have a different set of perceptions about how the organisation functions, i.e. what the dynamics at play are in the organisation.

Systems thinking, when applied to implementation strategies, has two levels. The first level is developing an understanding of the dynamics at play – this is the level at which causal loops are developed. The second level is refining the understanding of those dynamics. At this level, system archetypes are employed. System archetypes are structural patterns that appear in most organisations. A product of research into organisational dynamics, system archetypes represent the patterns of behaviour that are most often seen and felt within organisations of all types. Some of the archetypes that have been identified are Fixes that Fail, Limits to Growth, Shifting the Burden, and Accidental Adversaries. Let's start with these.

Fixes that Fail

In a 'Fixes that Fail' situation, a problem symptom cries out for resolution. A solution is quickly implemented which alleviates the symptom. However, the solution produces unintended consequences that, after a delay, cause the original problem symptom to return to its previous level or even get worse. This development leads us to apply the same (or similar) fix again. This reinforcing cycle of fixes is the essence of Fixes that Fail.

A key point to keep in mind about Fixes that Fail is that the problem symptom/quick fix/unintended consequence reinforcing process receives its energy directly from the implementation of the quick fix. Every time the quick fix is implemented, the unintended consequence loop is activated again. It is probably impossible to completely avoid Fixes that Fail because we can rarely know all the unintended consequences of our actions. However, through Fixes that Fail, we can begin to explore the unintended consequences of our actions before we implement them.

Here is an example of how Fixes that Fail really works. You are part of a management team that doesn't seem to be able to improve performance (problem symptom). You decide to yell at them to convince them to work harder to deliver (corrective action). On the surface, the threat should do it but, instead, they sink into a bunker mentality of fear of doing something wrong

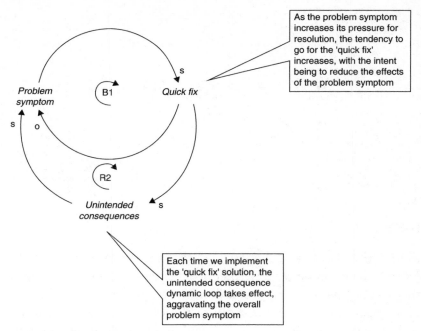

Figure 20 'Fixes that Fail'

(unintended consequence) and performance sinks even lower. The example is scary, but I have seen it happen.

Limits to Growth

In a 'Limits to Growth' scenario, growing actions initially lead to success which encourages even more of those efforts. Over time, however, the success itself causes the system to encounter limits, which slows down improvements in results.

As the success triggers the limiting action and performance declines, the tendency is to focus even more on the initial growing actions.

A great example of Limits to Growth was seen several years ago by Mr Gates' favourite software company, Microsoft. Microsoft's performance was spectacular. The better they did, the more

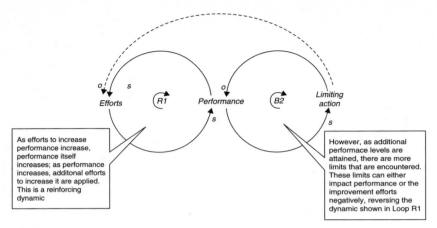

Figure 21 'Limits to Growth'

money they made and that enabled them to do even better still (efforts) to improve performance. But as they achieved everything that a CEO would want (total dominance in a market and never-ending resources), they ran afoul of the US government (limiting action) who took them to court. Although this little problem for Mr Gates is still not totally resolved, the court action will knock them down a bit, and either do damage to their performance or their efforts to improve it. Hard to believe, but sometimes our success is our own worst enemy.

Shifting the Burden

In a 'Shifting the Burden' situation, a problem symptom can be addressed by applying a symptomatic solution or a more fundamental solution. When a symptomatic solution is implemented, the problem symptom is reduced or disappears, which lessens the pressure for implementing a more fundamental solution.

Over time, the symptom resurfaces, and another round of symptomatic solutions is implemented in a vicious, figure-8 reinforcing cycle. The symptomatic solutions often produce

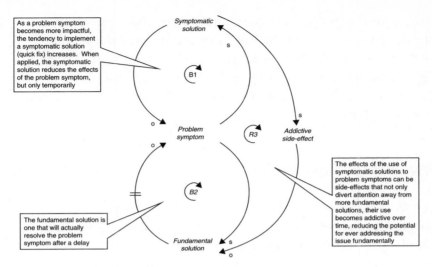

As a problem symptom becomes more impactful, the tendency to implement a symptomatic solution (quick fix) increases. When applied, the symptomatic solution reduces the effects of the problem symptom, but only temporarily

The fundamental solution is one that will actually resolve the problem symptom after a delay

The effects of the use of symptomatic solutions to problem symptoms can be side-effects that not only divert attention away from more fundamental solutions, their use becomes addictive over time, reducing the potential for ever addressing the issue fundamentally

Symptomatic solution

Problem symptom

Addictive side-effect

Fundamental solution

Figure 22 'Shifting the Burden'

side-effects that further divert attention away from more fundamental solutions.

Here is an example of Shifting the Burden that, although not pretty, does sum up how it works. Every couple of years, there is a major drought in middle Africa and with the drought comes stories of starving people. We have all seen the news stories and they are pretty sad. Starving people are the problem symptom, not the real problem, however. When we see these stories, we get concerned and are faced with a choice – to either help them with a symptomatic solution or a fundamental solution. We – the west – tend to go for the symptomatic solution of airlifting food and medical help in. This solution makes sense – we help the starving people by feeding them and helping to take care of them; and it makes us feel good. And, yes, it does go after the problem symptom. The other option would be to help them ensure that they don't have this problem ever again by teaching them better farming methods, ways to avoid over population, and other self-sufficiency methods. This too would go after the problem symptom, but it would take a lot longer. And they are starving today, so we usually go after the quick fix (symptomatic solution).

But with this choice comes an unintended consequence or two. In this case, as soon as the stories disappear from the news, we believe the problem has gone away and we tend to stop helping. This means that the fundamental solution will never be achieved and the problem will come back, every couple of years, just as it does.

Accidental Adversaries

In an 'Accidental Adversaries' scenario, two groups in an organisational population individually work to improve their performance. As the performance of either group increases, it increases their capacity, thereby increasing the combined performance. However, as each works to improve their performance, the act of reviewing performance can have a

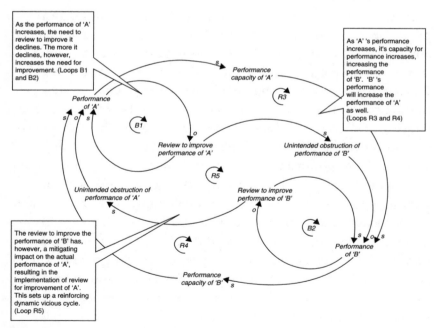

Figure 23 'Accidental Adversaries'

mitigating, although unintended, impact on the other. This unintended obstructive impact causes a reduction in the performance of the other group, resulting in a review for improvement. This, in turn, results in a similar impact on the initial group's performance.

Now, just because I really like the Accidental Adversaries archetype, I will share an example of how this was used really effectively. Here is the scenario – I was doing some work with a CEO who was faced with a pretty serious decision; should he install two VPs to run one of his divisions that he was reorganising. There were some pretty obvious pros and cons to the decision, but the archetype was used to surface some of the less obvious ones. Here is how it was used (I am going to show you a copy of the memo that was actually used, although I have changed the names for good reason).

The Risk of Accidental Adversaries in the new Acme organisational structure

One of tools that can be used to examine the potential benefits from decision making is a system dynamics archetype known as Accidental Adversaries. The archetype was identified by researchers at MIT's Organisational Learning Centre in the mid-1990s as one of the repetitive patterns of behaviour that occurs in organisations of all types and from all sectors. Basically, the archetype identifies how certain actions (variables) that take place have either a positive or negative effect on other variables in a system. Before reading on, it is important to focus on one thing: a system dynamic archetype identifies structure. It does not represent good or bad, but simply structure. And the rule is that 'structure drives behaviour'. So, therefore, if a structure exists in an organisation, it will be able to exhibit either good or bad behaviours, based on what inputs begin the structure to work.

In this memo, I will use the archetype as a template to examine the rationale behind either a single or dual leadership function for your new structure. Note: the archetype will show the relationship between the variables in the structure. The impact of the relationship is shown by either an 'S' or an 'O'. 'S' means 'same', i.e. as one variable increases (or decreases) in strength, it causes the next variable to increase (or decrease) in strength. 'O' means 'opposite', i.e. as one variable increases (or decreases) in strength, it causes the next variable to decrease (or increase) in strength.

The basic structure that you are trying to achieve is seen below.

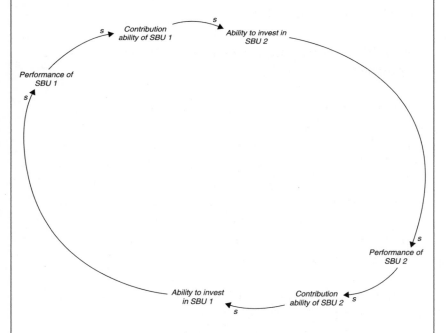

As can be seen in this diagram, you will have two SBUs, each a key unit of Acme. The intent is to create the two SBUs to leverage the ability of the organisation to perform. As each

SBU performs well, it will increase the ability of the SBU to contribute to the overall success of Acme. This success will, in turn, enable additional investments in the SBUs, thus reinforcing a virtuous cycle – success leads to additional success. This is good news, and is the basis for the plan to have two SBUs.

I believe that this model represents a single leadership point for the two SBUs. With a singular leadership point, you would be able to create an environment in which each SBU would be focused on their individual segments of the Acme business. This ability to focus on a business segment while under a single leader (with a singular focus on overall Acme performance) would enable the structure to build upon itself. The key here is ensuring that you have the right leader in place. As this diagram represents structure, you can see how negative performance in one SBU will begin to create problems for the other SBU and, consequently, overall Acme performance, i.e. as performance of one SBU goes down, it will reduce the ability of that SBU to contribute, reducing the ability of Acme to invest in either SBU. This structure turns from a virtuous cycle to a vicious cycle.

Now, let's make an assumption that you have the 'right' leader in place. The structure would then remain (or return) to exhibiting virtuous cycle behaviours.

Another option that you and I have discussed is to actually split the two SBUs into two separate business units, each led by a different person. When we then look at the structure, we begin to see a different outcome. If each SBU were led by a different person, it would undoubtedly begin to foster competition between the two business units. On the surface, competition could be good, driving each unit further to exceed targets. Competition between two business units in one organisation that has shared resources, however, can set up an Accidental Adversarial relationship between the two. This would create a different set of behaviours than are seen in the first structure. Note, this structure is the same, it only has additional elements that appear within it.

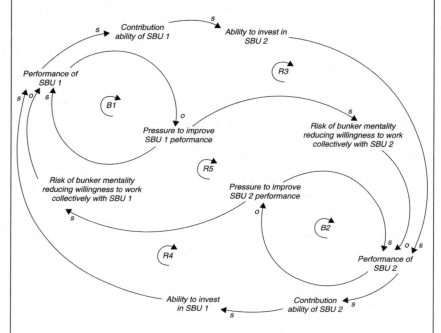

As each business leader begins to feel the pressure of competition for shared resources, you would run the risk of them falling into a 'bunker mentality' – a mentality in which their own survival and that of their SBU become more important than the overall performance of Acme. When a bunker mentality sets in, it causes a reduced ability of the other SBU to effectively utilise the resources that are shared by both. This will, in turn, begin to reduce the performance of each SBU, for the SBU that is feeling the impact of the other unit's bunker mentality will fall into this trap as well. The net result is that the overall structure shifts from exhibiting virtuous behaviours to one that exhibits vicious behaviours.

Once again, I must emphasise that what we are looking at are examples of potential structures that can impact Acme. The reason to use the archetypes to examine the structure is to see any potential impacts prior to the implementation of a policy decision. Based on what these structures show, it would seem to me that the best solution would be to have two SBUs, each with an SBU head, but one leader of Acme reporting to you. The biggest reason is the element of shared services by both the SBUs. The key will be to ensure that the leader who is selected has the skills, competency, passion and insights to lead the units effectively.

Do you have to use all these archetypes to avoid the problems that accompany poor performance? Of course not. As a matter of fact, you don't have to use any of them if you don't want to. You can choose to see good performance every once in a while if you want to. The only reason that I am showing them to you is that businesses cannot keep reliving the same problems year after year if they want to stay in business. And one good way of avoiding this is to use systems thinking to get a better grip on what is really going on, and what the unintended consequences are of our actions. Regardless how clever and cunning they may seem on the surface.

SYSTEMS THINKING – REVIEW

Purpose

Systems Thinking and causal loop diagrams are used to make explicit one's thinking about the dynamics at play in an organisation or an organisational system.

When to use

Systems thinking is especially powerful when there are concerns about the potential unintended consequences that may occur during the deployment and implementation of a new set of goals, initiatives or changes in an organisation.

Process

- Identify all the variables of the system in question.
- Determine the relationship between the variables.
- Determine the effect of those relationships.
- Validate the thinking that was used to develop the causal loop representation of the dynamics at play with additional population groups within the organisation.
- Draw conclusions based on the dynamics represented.
- Determine appropriate interventions and intervention techniques.

Audit Process

Any time an organisation tries to implement a new plan, it is important to audit the process. This is extremely important, because without an audit of the process, it will be impossible to determine if the process is accomplishing what it was designed to do. To conduct an effective audit, one needs to go back to the documentation of how the process was developed, i.e. the implementation strategy itself. The audit process should look at several things: what was trying to be accomplished, the actual implementation steps, the timelines that were set out for implementation, and the level of satisfactory accomplishment of those steps. All of this information can be clearly identified through the utilisation of an effectiveness matrix. The matrix that is most often used is one that was designed for Quality Function Deployment (QFD), which is a way to listen to the voice of the customer in all the quality management literature. The matrix, known in QFD terms as Chart A1, looks rather complex, but in reality, is nothing more than several matrices combined into one.

The effectiveness matrix can be broken into several pieces for ease of understanding.

Area A of the matrix is where the goal elements of the implementation are shown. In some cases, these might be the needs of a customer, in other cases, they might be the various dimensions of a new product. This area is commonly known as the 'whats'.

Area B is where the methods that are being used to satisfy the 'whats' are listed. These are commonly known as the 'hows'.

Area C is the place on the matrix (the cells) that will graphically show the relationship of the information in Area B to the key indicators in Area A. This is the relationship between the 'hows' and the 'whats'. Each relationship cell is divided diagonally to permit both a graphic representation of the relationship and a quantitative representation. The symbols used in this area are the same as in any other matrix – double circles, circles and triangles.

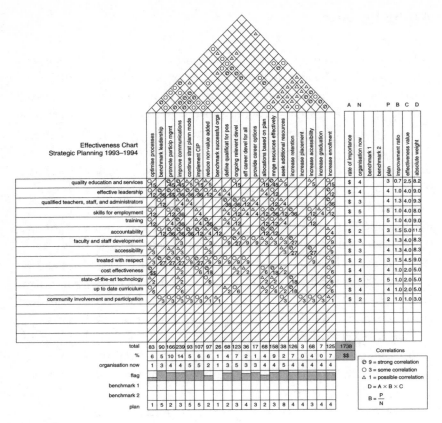

Figure 24 Effectiveness matrix

The quantitative values applied to the symbols are, double circle = 9, circle = 3, triangle = 1.

Area D is the area to show graphically the relationship between all of the 'hows' found in Area B. This will be critical, for some of the 'hows' – the actual activities to be performed – will have either a positive or negative effect on each other, resulting in either gain or loss from their use. Gains will be positive and will result in a higher level of indicator achievement; losses will require a reappraisal of that element of effort.

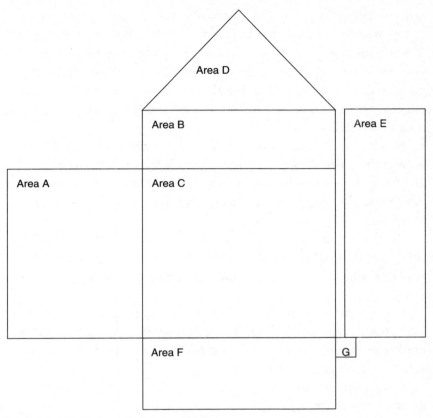

Figure 25 Effectiveness matrix breakdown

Area E consists of several components. 'Rate of importance' is a quantitative evaluation of the importance of each need found in Area A. The ranking is developed by the customers of the implementation initiative and is usually on a scale of 1–5, with 5 representing the strongest reason for the implementation, i.e. the strongest need. Although different members of an organisational population may rate specific needs in different rankings of importance, the composite group will establish the ranking order.

'Organisation now' is a quantitative evaluation of how the organisation is currently doing in satisfying the implementation requirements (Area A). The evaluation is done by a planning group with input from the larger organisational population. What is being looked for here is not necessarily high numbers, but numbers that reflect the reality of the situation. Once again, the ranking scale is 1–5, with 5 again representing the highest level of effectiveness response. These current effectiveness rankings are relative to each other.

'Benchmark 1' and 'benchmark 2' are available for quantitative evaluations of how other similar organisations are doing in satisfying the same implementation needs. These values are determined by the planning group with data supplied from the benchmarked organisations.

'Plan' is a quantitative evaluation of the current plan to address each specific implementation need. The numerical evaluation is based on the same 1–5 scale, and is determined by the planning group.

'Improvement ratio' is a mathematical function of 'Plan' divided by 'Organisation now'. This mathematical expression does not require additional input – it is just a formula that will result in a value for purposes of evaluation.

'Effectiveness value' is a mathematical function of 'Rate of Importance' multiplied by 'Importance ratio'. The purpose of this component is to further quantitatively measure the efforts of the organisation to deploy the implementation strategy.

Area F also consists of several components.

'Total' is the sum of all the mathematical values found in each column of Area B.

'%' is the proportion of each column total as divided by the total of all vertical columns.

'Organisation now' is a quantitative evaluation of how well the organisation is doing what it says it will do (the 'hows' found in Area B).

'Flag' is a graphic representation of the progress of the organisation in the completion of each method being used in the implementation.

'Benchmark 1' and 'benchmark 2' are quantitative evaluations of the efforts of other similar organisations conducting similar implementations.

Area G is for value totals. The main value in using the effectiveness matrix is to graphically show in one document how effective, or not effective, all the implementation strategies are.

Okay, so by now, some of you are saying to yourself, 'does he really expect me to use this thing?' Well, guess what? I don't really care if you use it or not. All I know is that I have used it and it works. It is a great way to easily show how well a plan is going. It is a great way to help someone (like your boss) know that you are doing what you set out to do, and that you are not just relying on information from employees who may or may not be doing the work.

Is it different from other ways you have shown the results of other planning assessments? Probably. But then again, I think I said earlier that learning new stuff is not all that bad. Your decision. After all, your company's success is your problem, not mine.

Strategy Checklist

1 Does your company have a strategy?
2 Has it been working? Has it been working as well as it could?
3 How often is the strategy reviewed? By whom?
4 Who provides input to the strategy development process?
5 Are customers and other stakeholders invited to participate?
6 Does your strategy include a comprehensive look at what scenarios your company may be facing?
7 Do your strategic goals all connect to the vision for the future of your organisation?
8 Are the goals prioritised, based on how much leverage each of them provides for the successful achievement of the vision?
9 Is the strategy available for all employees to see?
10 If the employees have questions or concerns about the strategy, is there a way that they can communicate them?
11 Does your strategic planning process take the ambiguity out of the questions, 'what should we do?' and 'how should we do it?'
12 Does your strategy allow for unforeseen events that can mitigate your ability to achieve the current goals?
13 If you felt that the strategic planning process needed improvement, is there a way to do this?
14 Is there a clear audit process to check strategic progress toward the vision?
15 Who does the auditing?

Frequently Asked Questions – Strategy

1 *Why is it that we never seem to be able to make our strategy work?*

This is a problem for many organisations today, and it stems largely from the fact that, whilst all strategies are supposed to work, the reality is that many of them simply cannot work. They are not based on the reality of the environment the company is in; they were not developed with the input of people who know what works and what doesn't work; they have too many goals; they have goals and targets that do not connect with where the organisation is trying to go; and the resources that will be needed to make the strategy work are not made available.

2 *Why can't I find out what our strategy is?*

There are usually three reasons for this: management has decided not to tell you; there was no communications plan put together by the people who made the plan; or you haven't bothered to ask. If management just hasn't decided to say anything, the plan is probably just a 'show' document to impress the public – not a good reason to go through all the effort of making one. If there is no communications plan, there is a good chance the plan will never work – strategies need to be disseminated, both internally and externally, in a rational, well-thought-out manner. A good communications plan should be developed before the strategy is implemented. And if you just haven't bothered to ask, then that would be a different problem. If you have asked, but can't get an answer, ask someone else.

3 *I don't see how my day-to-day work is affected by, or contributes to, our strategy.*

This usually signals that there isn't a communications plan to accompany the strategy. For a strategy to work, and to be effective, all employees need to see the connection between what they do in their usual jobs, and the strategic direction of the organisation. This is the only way (outside of hard-core coercion) to create the environment where employees will become motivated and committed to the strategic direction that has been selected.

4 *Where do the planners get these ideas?*

This question usually arises when the strategy doesn't make sense. Of all the things a strategy should represent, common sense should be very high on the list. Every strategic goal and target should be able to be tracked directly to progress toward the desired future of the company, i.e. the company vision. If the goals and targets do not track toward the vision, the goals are misguided, and will result in wasted time and resources; something in this time of increased competitive pressures few organisations can afford.

5 *Why does our strategy seem to keep changing?*

First, a strategy is nothing more than a plan to move an organisation toward its vision, and if the plan keeps changing, it is either a sign that the vision is changing (not a good sign), or that the previous plan wasn't good (a poor reflection on those who made it and approved it). My belief is that strategies should not change, but that they should evolve and be flexible enough to deal with changing organisational dynamics and the business environment the company finds itself in. However, there is a caveat to this last sentence; if the planners put appropriate effort into understanding the potential scenarios the company may find itself in, the plan should have taken those into account to begin with.

6 *How can we make sure that everyone in our company, who needs to know, really does understand our strategy?*

This question goes back to having a sound communications plan. And to clarify something; everyone in the company – from the CEO to the late-night shift clean up people – needs to know what the strategy is, and how their work will impact it. Employees are not the only ones who should understand the strategy and its implications. A sound strategy is one that involves, and is shared with, suppliers. There is no way a company will be able to achieve its strategic goals if its key suppliers are not onboard and committed to it.

7 *How does management expect us to do our day jobs and at the same time be responsible for some of the strategic initiatives?*

A fair question, and one that comes up quite often. When developing the strategy, consideration should be taken as to what can rationally be expected from employees and managers who will need to directly participate in the achievement of goals and targets. Quite often, this means dedicated releases to work on the strategy but, most often, it means just extra work, without any extra time to do it. This problem needs to be thought through whilst the plan is being developed, not dealt with when workload (and stress) issues surface. Many organisations that get this right build in reward structures for employees who are asked to put forth extra effort – reward structures that are based on recognition and other non-monetary direct compensation.

8 *Why is it that, quite often, our strategy seems to fall apart at the last minute?*

This is because the strategy was probably doomed to failure to begin with, usually because the plan didn't take potential scenarios into consideration, or the need for employee buy-in and commitment didn't have the appropriate resources required, or – and this can be a major problem – someone in the head offices decided to shift direction.

9 *What is the best method to use for strategic planning?*

Whilst there are more strategy methodologies out there than there are tourists in Mallorca in summer, what always seems to win out is a strategy that is based on common sense; has input from managers, employees, suppliers and customers; takes into consideration potential scenarios that the company may encounter; tracks directly to the company vision; has a sound communications plan; and gets employees fired up to make it successful.

part II

Performance

04

The Impact of Personal Performance

How to improve your personal performance to act as a role model

One of the most often heard frustrations in organisations today is the belief that change seems to be becoming constant. The change being talked about directly impacts organisational performance, whether on an individual or collective level. With all the ongoing talk about the need to reduce costs, the main drive of the change effort seems to target reorganisation. Reorganisation itself has become a service industry, a focus for authors, and so entrenched in our culture, we tend to expect that our organisations will be reorganised over and over again.

The intent of most reorganisations is to help the subject organisation become more effective at delivering consistent high performance. However, the evidence of long-term increases in performance improvement is minimal. This can be due to either the lack of sufficient time to measure results, or the short-term focus of the efforts. What is becoming apparent is that the level of stress among the people affected by the change is increasing. Appropriate questions might be, why then does it seem that many senior managers are becoming addicted to constant organisational change, and what has all this change done to really impact performance?

There are many reasons to implement, or try to implement, a performance-driven reorganisation plan. These include an organisation's perceived inability to compete in the marketplace, the perceived level of organisational effectiveness, the organisational ability to obtain the resources it believes it needs to exist, and the organisation's perceived ability to plan strategically. In all these situations, the key element is the organisation's 'perception' of itself. There is a connective relationship between an organisation's perception of itself and its ability to understand its current reality. Unfortunately, some senior managers – the people who theoretically have overall organisational responsibility – appear to believe that they have a better view of this relationship.

As an organisation's perceptions of itself drift from its reality, several dynamics begin to take place. These dynamics can be characterised by the mental models that become acted out by the employees of the organisation. These mental models include, *'we will never be effective at performance improvement if we keep changing'*, *'how can we increase accountability with constant change'*, and *'are we still headed in the same direction as we were?'*

We Will Never Be Effective If We Keep Changing

This mental model can result in a diminished ability on the part of the employees to work as effectively as they can. This dynamic is not unusual. Until the late 1950s, it was a common belief that man could not run a mile in less than four minutes. This belief was reinforced by the fact no one had done so. When Roger Bannister broke the four-minute barrier, suddenly others began to run a mile in less than four minutes – the belief that it could not be done was broken by the evidence that it could be done. Through an example of a successful attempt, more success could be achieved.

In organisations, if we begin to believe that we will not be able to perform better due to ongoing reorganisation efforts, the end result will be reduced performance. Without appropriate benchmarks of success that can be quantified and qualified, people will feel that they are being put in a vicious circle of increased chaos. Effectiveness is a function of knowing where the organisation is going, how it is to get there, and what part we all play in that movement. As the addiction to ongoing change increases, the potential for organisational effectiveness and consistent high performance will decrease.

How Can We Increase Accountability With Constant Change?

Accountability in organisations is usually defined as being evaluated on what we do and how well we do it. In an organisation that is undergoing constant, ongoing change, it can be difficult to know what to do and, therefore, how to do it. Additionally, as organisations move their employees from division to division or shuffle old employees out and new ones in, the ability to know who is to do what is diminished. As we move people from one area to another while effectiveness efforts are underway, they will have a tendency to fall back into old ways of doing business – no rewards for effectiveness will lead to reduced effectiveness activity. Addiction to organisational change as a way to do business will decrease the potential for accountability in the organisation.

Are We Still Headed in the Same Direction We Were?

An ongoing problem in many organisations is the loss of organisational 'history'. It is the history, or organisational memory, that can keep an organisation from reliving many of the mistakes that they face over and over again. When the organisation loses much of its capacity for retaining the history of the organisation, it is not only doomed to relive the same mistakes over again, it can find itself being pulled and driven by both internal and external political influences. These influences have a tendency over time to change the stated direction or vision of the organisation in a de-facto manner. The organisational vision may remain constant, but the actions that the organisation takes are in opposition to the stated vision, i.e. they are congruent with the organisational influences but not with the organisational collective knowledge. The addiction to change will decrease the ability to see and understand the long-term vision for an organisation.

A result of these mental models and the actions they stimulate can be a belief on the part of senior management that the employees of an organisation are not competent, nor have the capacity to help move an organisation forward, resulting in less performance effectiveness.

This result will increase the addiction to constant organisational change. Addiction to reorganisational change causes increased evidence of these mental models and their subsequent actions, leading to more organisational change. The outcome can be a belief that the senior management of an organisation is literally leading the change for the sake of keeping enough fluidity to reinforce their position as the only ones who can lead the organisation. The dynamics of ongoing change are relatively easy to see. The driver to change is usually a belief on the part of senior management that the organisation is not as effective as it should be.

The belief is that the less effective an organisation appears to be, the more senior management uses reorganisation as a technique to remedy the situation, and as the reorganisation efforts increase, the organisation should become more effective and, therefore, the less the organisation should need to reorganise. Unfortunately, there is strong reason to believe that simple reorganisation is a 'quick-fix' remedy, and its effects may not last over time.

A long-term more sustainable solution to a gap in the desired level of organisational effectiveness and the current reality is the development of measures of effectiveness that are based in reality. This is a key point. If measures of effectiveness are simply pulled from the air, their potential will be nil. Developing measures of effectiveness, and holding the organisation accountable for their achievement, will have the tendency to act as a long-term fundamental solution, not simply another quick fix.

When both of these options for increasing organisational effectiveness are plotted together, it is clear that there is a serious level of addiction to doing what managers have done all along. The more senior management opts for reorganisation as a method for increasing effectiveness (a short-term quick fix), the less stable the organisation will be. This lack of stability can lead to the belief on the part of senior management that the organisational population is not capable of becoming more effective, and this will lead to a reinforcement of the belief of the need for someone who can 'save' the organisation. The saviour of choice of senior management is, of course, senior management. If this behaviour falls into place, there would be no reason to implement reality based measures, for the mental model in play is that the staff competency level is low and, therefore, not worth measuring. Having no way to actively measure effectiveness, the organisation falls back into reorganisation as the technique of choice for increasing effectiveness, again providing reinforcement for the addictive behaviours of senior management.

As the addiction to organisational change grows, the mental models of the people affected by the changes tend to solidify. They include:

- It doesn't do any good to try to put forth an extra effort.
- Lack of knowledge is the real key to the problem.
- Constant change inhibits the potential for reorganisation efforts to become effective.
- We are just reliving 'quick-fix' actions of the past.
- Political influences are driving the change process.
- Chaos never allows real accountability to be evaluated.
- It is easier to blame than to learn.
- Pitting people against each other through blame eliminates putting forth extra effort.
- Questioning change efforts is extremely risky professionally, and can result in either public humiliation, the appearance of not being on the 'team', or possible termination.

The addictive dynamics of ongoing organisational change can result in several things. All will have a long-term detrimental impact on the organisation and its potential over time for several reasons.

First, constant ongoing change creates a situation in which people rarely stay in a department or division long enough for any change efforts to take effect. This results in the loss of organisational history, which in turn leads to reliving organisational mistakes. Without the ability to 'remember' the organisational past, corporations and institutions will make costly avoidable mistakes.

Second, constant organisational change sets up the belief that few in the organisation have knowledge as to what the next change will be, nor what the overall plan for change will be. Without a collective understanding of the 'big picture' about why increased performance is needed, it becomes more difficult to expect that the organisational population will be able to work collectively to help move the organisation forward to achieve its goals and vision.

Third, in conjunction with the previous characteristic, constant organisational change helps reinforce the organisational power structure. This is due to the lack of understanding or knowledge as to the overall change direction and plan. Consequently, there is the belief that some organisational power structures keep stirring the organisational pot to retain organisational control.

Fourth, constant organisational change leads to the ability of external forces to exert political pressure on senior management that can lead to knee-jerk reactions that are not in the best interests of the long-term future of the organisation, its employees and stakeholders.

The impact of addiction to organisational change leads to behaviours that are parallel to other forms of addiction. More traditional addictions lead to feelings of worthlessness, remorse, incompetence and the belief that everything is out of one's control. In the case of organisational addiction to change, the evident behaviours are similar.

Traditional symptoms	Management/organisational symptoms
Loss of connectedness to others	Lack of support and buy-in
Feelings of worthlessness	Not adding value to organisational efforts
Blame on others	Fractionalisation of organisational efforts
Fear of loss of addiction	Loss of power and control
Out of control life patterns	Disconnect to organisation
Don't care, just need the 'fix'	Rapid changes

When implementing change in organisations, senior management should consider several lessons.

Make change efforts visible. Not communicating the rationale, method and plans for change will reduce the ability of the organisation to buy-in and support the change efforts.

Develop clear measures of accountability. Even in the midst of change, it is crucial to enable an organisational population to be able to see how they will be held accountable for the success of the change efforts.

Increase input from employees. A key element to organisational change efforts is the input from all employee levels that will be impacted by the changes. Without high levels of input, the efforts will be only those of senior management and the level of active buy-in will be reduced.

Stay focused on the organisational vision. The connection of reorganisational efforts to the organisational vision will be key to the success of the efforts and the level of organisational buy-in.

Be consistent in dealing with employees. When employees feel that they are being treated differently than others, the organisational climate will suffer, reducing the potential for reorganisational success.

Look at the long-term ramifications of change efforts. Developing quick-fix answers to problems is easy, but developing long-term solutions to fundamental organisational problems requires an examination of both the short and long-term impact on the organisation.

In this time of increasing competition and decreasing availability of resources, having organisations become more effective is crucial. However, the methods for becoming more effective need to be examined prior to any change efforts. Senior management is traditionally held responsible for the success of organisations, and success should be measured over long periods of time, not just the next quarter.

The Desert Group: A Case Study of Performance in Action

Organisations face many problems, but of them all, two could be the most impactful; how to grow a business, and how to ensure that the growth helps the organisation become sustainable over time. As organisations grow, they experience several things. As growth occurs, organisations find themselves facing the challenge of increasing employee skills, increasing the company's ability to reinvest in its infrastructure, and increasing the level of customer satisfaction. At the same time, companies need to be able to reduce costs and ensure that they don't lose sight of their long-term vision for their future. Recently, a service organisation in America began to feel the impact of these dynamics.

The service organisation, for the purposes of this I will call it the Desert Group, was a self-supporting division of an international organisation. Their core business was consulting to other organisations on various business topics. Although the Desert Group was relatively young, they had made great strides in the past several years – growing from 15 people in 1996 to over 125 in 1999. The senior partners in the group had postured their business very well. They had set their business goals based on what they believed were specific customer needs – the need to reduce third-party spend funds through outsourcing services.

As the company had grown, the partners were able to bring in two types of employees – young business school graduates and older, experienced hires. The decision of how to blend the new employees was based on both access to financial resources, and the need to ensure that the skill level of the employees was a combination of the latest theory and hands-on experience in outsourcing. As the company began to grow, it became more credible – a key to growth: credibility leads to additional visibility, which in turn leads to more business. The relationship between these business variables was the foundation for the Desert Group's growth engine.

Even though these interrelationships were the group's growth engine, their ability to hire and retain qualified employees also became a key limit to their continued growth.

As an organisation becomes more credible in the marketplace, its business will grow more – as it grows, it will become more credible. However, as it grows, the business will need to hire more qualified staff to deal with the new business. But as this need increases – as an organisation struggles to find the 'right people' – the organisation's ability to perform consistently will decrease and, therefore, decrease its ability to grow.

In the case of the Desert Group, this limit became real very quickly. In addition, other dynamics that were affected by the limit also came into play. As the senior partners of the group worked to continue their strategic gains by building an infrastructure to enable them to hire effectively, they began to encounter several potential negative dynamics that, if they were permitted to continue, would act as additional limits to growth. These additional dynamics included: the growing organisation's ability to 'stay the course', i.e. build a common shared vision of what they were attempting to accomplish; the effectiveness of employees; how to build a growing leadership infrastructure while meeting the day-to-day requirements of meeting client needs; and the potential that the parent organisation might 'pull the plug'.

Shared vision

The organisation and its potential future was the vision of one of the initial partners in the group. The vision was two-fold – not only was the vision a picture of what the group could be, it was the belief that the group would be able to accomplish what it was trying to accomplish. Communicating a vision to what seemed to be an ever-changing organisational population group became a challenge in itself.

As the group grew, its ability to ensure that all the new employees would be able to 'see the same picture' became critical. More employees meant a great potential for diffusion of the vision. Additionally, as the group grew in size, the potential that many of the new employees would even believe that the group could become what the senior partners saw became diminished. This required a substantial effort being placed on building organisational alignment with the vision. If the level of organisational alignment with the vision would drop too low – beyond an intangible perceived level of acceptability – the group's long-term potential would be mitigated. They could still become an effective organisation, but not become what the partners saw as a future.

Varying employee perceptions

Every time a new employee was hired, the organisation had to deal with the 'baggage' that the employee brought with them to the group. For the new hires, this was manageable. The new hires were largely from business schools, full of theories and concepts of how a business should work, but with little or no real working experience. This lack of real experience became a drain on effectiveness, as the existing experienced employees were forced to reduce client contact time in order to help the new hires 'mature' in the organisation, and in business in general. This loss of effective performance was counter intuitive. The common belief in business is that the most effective way to increase productivity peformance is to hire additional employees. By using a business simulation model, the partners were able to 'test' their mental models of the most effective way in which to increase effectiveness – by hiring a large number of people quickly, the existing employee effectiveness dropped further due to their need to mentor and coach than it did by hiring new employees at a slower rate.

Through the use of an orientation programme for new hires, the management would be able to create and instill the view of an effective organisation. Experienced hires presented a different problem, however. There would be a delay in the overall productivity effectiveness of the experienced hires, not only due to working in a new system, but also due to the potential belief patterns of how a business should function. As more experienced hires were brought onboard, the group began to experience more and more disconnects in alignment in thinking. There were few potential hiring pools of people who had worked in a similar environment, and as each experienced hire came onboard, the partners experienced a reduction in their productivity due to time they had to spend helping 'paint' the picture of how the business would, and should, function.

Leadership infrastructure

Building a leadership infrastructure is something that most organisations shy away from. This can be due to either a lack of understanding of the need for it, or a perceived inability to take the time to do it. Leadership in the Desert Group meant leadership on all levels. The partners believed that if the organisation were to be truly effective, each employee would need to become a leader. Leadership did not translate into 'the people at the top of the hierarchy', but instead, 'anyone who was willing to help create an organisational environment in which all the employees could realise their own personal potential while working in an organisational structure'.

Being a leader meant being able to make sound decisions as to the priorities needed to run a business. With the organisation growing at the pace it was, recognising the need to mentor new employees while at the same time meeting current and future client needs was paramount. It became quickly apparent that the ability to prioritise time was a growing gap in the organisation.

Meetings for a growing leadership team were becoming increasingly difficult to schedule – both partners and staff were constantly feeling drawn to clients, either for implementing client solutions or soliciting new client engagements. And, too often, when meetings were scheduled the majority of staff who were suppose to attend were absent.

Several retreats were scheduled to discuss the organisational vision and to build alignment within the group, but even these activities proved to be not as effective as desired. With the group growing at the rate it was, the leadership group kept expanding at a pace that required 're-inventing the wheel' of building the leadership infrastructure. Clearly, the growth pattern was causing problems for the group.

The potential of losing control

The parent company was pleased with the group's growth. After only several years of working together, the group had already become the most profitable group in the overall organisation. This in itself was a mixed blessing. Success breeds the expectation of continued success, and the parent company continually set higher goal expectations for the group. These expectations came in the form of growth targets, both for headcount and revenue generation.

The rewards that came with success were substantial, but with the success also came increased levels of stress. The stress manifested itself in several ways, but the highest stress came from the increasing potential to make mistakes that the parent company would view as unacceptable. Many organisations have recognised the need to create a 'safe place' that is conducive to exponential growth patterns. A safe place is one that is defined as a place in which it is okay to make mistakes – not mistakes that can be terminal for an organisation, but mistakes that the organisation can learn from. The feeling was that on a group level, mistakes were acceptable. The group believed that the parent organisation did not have the same belief pattern. The parent company had a history of not making mistakes (or at least not making them visibily), and the fear was that if too many mistakes were made, it would result in a decrease in the growth pattern and, consequently, an intervention from the parent company. To avoid a potential intervention, the Desert Group personnel worked and over-worked themselves to keep up.

As the Desert Group grew, it hired additional staff, both new hires and experienced hires. The additional staff required additional time spent mentoring and, consequently, time away from doing what they were hired to do, which was client work. This reduced the overall performance of the organisation, which would in turn reduce the growth of the business itself. As the growth of the business would decline, the potential for parental intervention would increase. This, in turn, would reduce the level of leadership infrastructure in the group, reducing the number of people in the company that had bought into the group's vision. This would increase the need to spend time with employees' mentoring which would reduce overall performance even further. This entire situation became a vicious cycle. Once it began, there would be no way to stop it.

Group interventions

To lessen the potential impact of what might happen, the partners began to develop a series of interventions. Some of the interventions were meant to deal with existing dynamics, while others were designed to reduce the potential for negative impacts in the future. The interventions were classified into four groups; improving the core competencies of the managers, creating an environment conducive for the managers to learn the benefits of group empowerment, making explicit the need to understand the differences between importance and urgency, and enhancing leadership performance.

Core competencies

It was determined that everyone in the Desert Group should have a set of core competencies – competencies that, when together, can provide high leveraged capacity to be an effective leader. These competencies, Thinking, Influencing, Achieving and Leading, are central to effective performance. Vision is the ability to develop and identify with a personal and organisational future. Understanding is the ability to have a shared belief as to why an organisational population acts in the way that they do. The ability to think and re-think about the interrelationships between actions and outcomes; the ability to influence others to see the benefits of performance-enhancing initiatives; the ability to achieve the goals and targets that are set out in a strategy; and the ability to demonstrate real leadership, are all critical if an organisation is going to be able to realise its potential.

It should be recognised that the competencies are not static or fixed – there is no 'set' way in which to ensure that a managerial or employee group acquires these skill sets. The competencies are fluid and dynamic in their interrelationship. Without these core competencies, it is doubtful that the Desert Group would be able to ensure that they can continue to flourish in the business opportunity environment they were facing.

Empowerment

Empowerment in any organisation is a topic that is laced with confusion and misunderstanding. No one can create empowerment, no one can give empowerment, no one can bestow empowerment. Empowerment is something that each of us chooses either to have or not have. Yes, management does have the 'power' to either empower or not, but the reality is that empowerment is something that we choose to take advantage of by demonstrating the willingness to perform. The Desert Group employees could choose to make decisions based on the belief that the decisions they make are appropriate because it is *their* firm, not because they had stock in the company, but because they supported and were committed to where the company was going. Without this sense of ownership, work remains work. With this sense of ownership, work becomes a positive experience, a feeling of connected responsibility for their collective future. Real empowerment is an outcome of shared vision – shared vision as to where an organisation is going and how it is going to get there.

Importance vs. Urgency

Urgency is a pressure that we usually impose upon ourselves. We can be told to do something right away because it is urgent, but it is our belief that urgency is more critical than importance that makes our decision. If the Desert Group was to be able to realise its vision, it must shift from the mindset of urgency before importance to one of importance first. If this shift does not occur, the practice will continue to play 'catch-up' when trying to increase the speed and effectiveness with which it can learn.

Leadership

Leadership is many things to many people. And, in most cases, the list of what it is is only exceeded by the list of what we think it is. One definition that is becoming more clearly recognised as being 'on target' is that leadership is 'the creation of an environment in which an organisational population can become effective'. This definition is important because it does not articulate anything specifically. That is why the definition is so important.

Leadership is not telling people what to do. It is not saying this is the appropriate direction for us to go. It is not about command and control. Leadership is all about helping others to develop their own understanding of what is important in helping an organisation move toward its vision. Leadership is all about helping others realise their potential.

Leadership has both direct and indirect relationships with other variables that impact organisational learning and productivity. As leadership actions improve, trust in managers and their ability to make sound decisions increases. This improves the organisational climate, which leads to increased sharing and open communications. This, in turn, increases the potential for leadership learning. Additionally, as the climate improves, there is less fear of risk taking and, consequently, more risk taking, again improving the level of trust. This positively impacts the belief on the part of the employees that work and learning can go together. This reduces the potential sense of negativity, increasing the climate even further. This model was developed as part of a research project into how organisational leadership impacts the organisation – the story was appropriate for the research, and it was appropriate for the Desert Group.

When exploring leadership, there are several things to consider. These include:

❑ Daniel Goleman, in his book titled *Emotional Intelligence*, says that being a 'people person' requires self-awareness and includes not only knowing yourself, but also knowing what motivates you and how you feel. This also includes mastering your own impulses, and the ability to listen, communicate, coach and reach out. These are 'qualities' of a good leader.

❑ Leaders focus on results, set clear expectations, steward progress and hold people accountable.

❑ Leadership is helping you develop your vision and your strategy. Leaders help you to have the proper structure in place to move in the direction you've chosen.

❏ Leadership is all about helping to keep the entrepreneurial spirit without being destroyed by bureaucracy.
❏ A leader understands that strategy is an idea, not an implementation.
❏ A leader does not create fear in the workplace.

The story of the Desert Group is one that many organisations go through. However, as many organisations just revert to old behaviours when facing complex decisions – as in the case of the Desert Group when trying to hold on to and improve performance – the barriers to performance improvement can be substantial.

03

Achieving

Achieving is what most managers focus on . . . getting it done; hitting those numbers; making it happen. And that is fine; after all, without achieving, there isn't much that counts in business. Or so most people think.

Achieving is usually measured by a 'tick in the box' – 'Did he get the job done?' Yes? No? Tick the right box. That is all fine, but there is a hard way to get things done and an easy way to do the same. I tend to believe that the easy way makes the most amount of sense, and because of that, I have put together a group of stories about how to do just that.

Is There an Easy Way to Survive Change?

Well, yes. The easiest way to survive change is to just go with it. After all, change is a given, and when managers and employees don't like it, one piece of advice they can receive is to 'get over it'. This is the reality of it all, but this kind of advice won't make change go any easier.

When an organisation's senior management makes the decision to implement a massive change programme, it needs to take many things into consideration. One of the things that are most important – and usually missed – is that organisations undergoing change are populated by three groups of people who will struggle with it all. These three groups are, those who don't know what to do, those who don't have the skills to do it, and those who don't want to change.

People who don't know what to do are those who, for some reason, have not seen nor heard about what is going on, or why. Sure, if you listen to senior managers, *everyone* has been told about the new initiative or change in direction. But the reality is that few communication efforts go as planned. There is an explanation for this. Many organisations, when contemplating the change effort, put as much effort into developing a communications plan as they do on planning the effort itself. Fine, you are saying, the change effort is clearly more important than the communications around it, but this is wrong. Look at it this way – if the 'effort' is going to be to change the performance of an organisation, and an organisation is made up of people, then it stands to reason that the behaviours that will have to shift are those of the people . . . and if they don't know what will happen, what the expectations of them are, or why all this will happen, there is little chance that they will know what to do. An effective communications plan can provide extremely high leverage to ensure that all the energy put into the change effort is not wasted. And even more important, if the entire organisational population clearly understands what is going to happen and why, the chances that some of them will try to resist the effort will be reduced.

The employees who don't have the skill sets to support the change are a different issue. The entire issue of having the 'right skills' to adapt to and support the change effort is a function of two things: what skills are needed, and what skills are currently residing in the organisation. When the change effort is planned, it is important to determine what skills will be needed to ensure that there won't be delays in achieving the goals of the plan. This is something else that is usually missed when mapping out a change strategy. Will the employees need to have additional people skills? Will they need additional technical skills? Does the company have people on staff who are capable of deploying the training? Will the company need to go 'outside' to supplement the needed training? Does the company have the funds available to do the training needed? What are the contingencies that might arise during the training? What are some of the unintended consequences of training? Of not doing the training? These questions are all very important and need to be considered prior to a plan being deployed.

And then there is the issue of what skills are currently in the company. Perhaps the easiest way to do this is to conduct a skills survey. This survey does not need to be done with all the employees, but it most certainly needs to be done with all the managers who will be charged with 'making it all happen'. A good skills survey looks at both technically oriented skills and the skills that we normally associate with human interactions. The 'people' skills are, in reality, the ones that can make or break a change effort. The ability to demonstrate high communications skills, the ability to coach effectively, the ability to help others see a potential desired future are all key people skills. And if a manager doesn't have those skills, any amount of technical skills will not carry the day. Being able to identify the current managerial skill level and then compare it to the needed level can point out any gaps that might be present – and will need to be filled if the change effort is to be successful.

Dealing with those employees who just don't want to change is another issue entirely. The rule of thumb is that most organisations consist of about 10 per cent of employees who 'don't get it' who will not want to change. When 'resistors' to change are encountered, there only are two options. First, make sure they do understand the what, why and how of the change effort. Make sure they have the skills they will need – if they don't, help them obtain them. If they still resist the change, then option two comes into play. Enable them to resist change in some other organisation. Change resistors are like a virus in an organisation and keeping them around will result in more problems in the future.

Surviving change is not easy. Change, especially when it is not your idea, can be stressful at best. But it is important to recognise that regardless of what we want, or what we do, change is a constant; one of the few constraints there are in business.

Those who try to resist change are most probably the same people who, as children, picked up their ball and ran home when they didn't like the rules of the game. Well, the principle rule of the business game is to survive.

Survival is a choice. And surviving it the easy way – by becoming part of the change – is better than trying to survive it the hard way – by resisting it.

Questions

- Do your company's employees perceive change to be a necessary evil or a parameter of business?
- Is change perceived to be just one more programme that will be over at some point?
- Why do employees find change so difficult to deal with at times?
- What could make this easier?

The Recipe for Getting It Right

All decision makers worry about getting it right the first time. And they should. And lately, we have seen evidence that it is getting harder and harder to do it. Just ask Rod Eddington. After a disastrous set of events, Mr Eddington was quoted as saying, 'the shambles . . . just set us right back and clearly we've got to work our way through that, learn the lessons and move on'. The reporter who interviewed him ('BA at breaking point?' *Daily Telegraph*, 29 August 2004) went on to say that, 'Eddington freely admits . . . that appropriate decisions were not taken at the right time'. Really.

There is no doubt that Rod Eddington has a difficult job – his airline British Airways has been hit by industrial actions, escalating fuel prices, the security fears around air travel after 9/11, air traffic control computer problems, staffing shortages, and fearsome competition from the discount airlines. And whilst all this has been going on, he has been working to cut costs by reducing the workforce, which certainly hasn't gone over well with the unions that populate the airline. No wonder his job is difficult; but what he is up against is not just a BA or an airline problem.

Getting it right – especially getting it right the first time – is a major challenge to business executives. And believe it or not, there is a recipe to do it. The first part of the recipe is to not believe that you have all the right answers. Too often, just because some manager works his way up to one of those posh offices, he begins to think that he 'knows' better than anyone else what to do. Well, maybe some of them do, but the problem ensues when they begin to believe it. Believing you 'have all the answers' causes many business executives to stop listening to the people who do the actual work. I used to write speeches for a CEO, and in one of them, I had inserted, 'neither I nor (his VP) have all the answers'. And he said it in front of 120 managers. Yes, he was pretty upset with me until he found out that his managers, for the first time, respected him for being open and honest. Knowing what to do is one thing; thinking you are the only one who knows is a real problem.

Second, it is crucial to think about some of the unintended consequences of your decision(s). All decisions have unintended consequences – some are great; some can lead to complete disaster. If you don't think about what they could be, you can wake up one morning to discover that the best of intentions were not enough. Oh, by the way, when you think of what else might happen, make sure you don't do it on your own. If you are making decisions that impact front line workers, try talking to some of them to find out how they might react. I am not saying that negative reactions should preclude you making the decision – sometimes hard decisions need to be made, regardless of the downside. What I am saying is make sure you know what else might happen before you do it. Adverse reactions to decisions are not bad news. Not knowing what the reactions will be is bad news.

Third, recognise that regardless of how sound your 'plan' appears on paper, it isn't worth anything if you can't make it work. In the case of BA, part of the 'plan' was to drastically reduce the workforce, whilst keeping the planes flying and the customers happy. Well, as we have seen in a couple of weeks in August 2004, there must have been some 'gaps' between the 'plan' and the reality. Yes, the company was able to cut over 13,000 jobs, yes, the company was able to save tons of money; but they had to cancel many flights and alienated many customers. So what happened? Weren't any scenarios developed that explored 'what if . . . ' situations? Didn't anyone plan for contingencies? Making sure the plan actually can work is pretty important to do I guess.

Fourth, be conscious of the fact that your ability to do what you are paid to do will depend not only on your skills, but also upon the 'team' of people who work for you. Too many times, when 'problems' arise from decisions, executives lean on their managers to sort them out. Good logic – these people are paid a lot to do what needs to be done. But quite often, the reasons that the decision didn't work out as you had planned are because of the abilities of those same people. And the folly of it all is that in many cases, these are the same people who are then made responsible to 'clean up the mess'. How can we expect people who contributed to the 'mess' to clean it up? Eddington's quote in the interview was, 'Let's be clear that the management team is going to take stock and review the lessons of last week'. Time will tell.

Being a CEO is tough work. But, as I recall, that is why they get paid so much – to be able to deal with the difficult decisions. And in all fairness to Mr Eddington, he has gotten it right in the past. Several months ago, he was the CEO who, with two of his direct reports, gave up their performance bonuses – even though they had hit their performance targets – because he had been asking his employees to take major financial hits during the cost cutting that was taking place at the airline. Which leads me to the fifth element of the recipe to get it right – act like a leader. You know, 'walk the talk'. When you are making tough decisions that will negatively impact the front line workers, make sure that you and your direct reports feel some pain. This is just common sense. If the front line workers believe that they are at the bad end of a double standard, your ability to do what needs to be done will be zip, zero, zilch, nada, nichts, rien, niente, or as a CEO once said to me, 'mildly impossible' – recipe or no recipe.

Questions

- Who does the actual planning in your organisation?
- Where do they get their input from?
- Are the plans they make realistic?
- Does your management team believe that 'the plan' must be followed at all cost, regardless of changing business environments and situations? Regardless of new opportunities?

Sitting on the Sidelines

I am not the world's greatest sports fan, but I do remember what it was like to go to a football match and sit in the stands with friends watching all the action on the pitch. And you know something? Every time I have done this, I have noticed something happening near me. The people I was with would tend to watch the match and then proffer advice on how the players should have played. Bad tackle, poor ball handling, sloppy footwork . . . the list goes on and on. And the same thing happens in the office. We sit on the sidelines and then make comments about other people's actions. Poor deployment, bad meeting facilitation, sloppy workmanship . . . and on and on. So what is it that causes people to make observations about the actions of others, especially in the case of work, instead of offering to assist? Is it better to just sit on the sidelines and snipe away at our peers? Do we for some reason like to see others become relegated to the scrap heap of apparent incompetents?

Sitting on the sidelines can be great fun, and clearly it is safer than being in the midst of the action, but in the realm of business, it is something that some might consider to reflect a lack of commitment to success. In organisations, just as in any team play, the only way success happens is when everyone is in the game. Now it is clear that 'being in the game' for some people may mean out on the pitch, for some it might be keeping the team fit, for some it might be selling tickets, and for some it might be cheering from the stadium. Regardless, each of these people 'are in the game'. We all need to recognise that real success doesn't occur when some people become so risk-adverse that they would rather just sit and wait it out until they know what side to cheer for. That represents politics in the workplace to the n'th degree. And when that type of environment is around you, no one will win over time.

Winning in business means not only 'hitting the numbers', but it also means that everyone *wants* to participate in the journey toward success. It means that everyone needs to 'see' the desired 'end goal' and do whatever they can to achieve it. It means that sitting on the sidelines should not be allowed. Think of the last time you were in a 'meeting before the real meeting'. You know, these are the 'meetings' that take place over coffee where people discuss what they think will happen in the real meeting. Think of what was being talked about. It is those conversations where you can tell who you are working with, and there really are only four types of employees who go to meetings.

Some people go to meetings as 'prisoners'. You know – a prisoner is someone who is attending the meeting because they have been told to be there. They have other things they would like to, or should do, but their boss has said they need to go, so they go. So they sit on the sidelines. Some people are there as 'vacationers'. A vacationer is someone who attends the meeting because it is better than doing what they really should or could be doing. So they sit on the sidelines. Some people go as 'sophisticates'. A sophisticate is someone who believes that they know more than anyone else in the meeting. They could do the facilitation better, they could make a better presentation, they could have drawn on better data. They think they know it all, and they sit on the sidelines. And then there are 'explorers'. An explorer is someone who may know something about a topic, or may know nothing about it at all, but in either case, are keen to learn as much as they can. 'Explorers' are rarely found sitting on the sidelines – they want to become involved, to participate, to learn and share, because that is what exploring is all about.

These four categories of people do not exhibit these characteristics because they have them in their DNA. Rather, they exhibit these characteristics because of their ability to make choices. We all have the ability to decide which type of employee we will be. We can decide that whilst we have other things to do, when told to attend a meeting, we can make the conscious choice to take it as an opportunity to learn something. We can decide that whilst we think that attending the meeting is better than doing our 'day job responsibilities', what we learn in the meeting just might help us do our day job better and easier. We can decide that, whilst we may be pretty smart about many things, being in the meeting *and* actively participating may help others learn what we know. These decisions are all part of learning and sharing . . . the key to being an explorer.

I am not advocating everyone being on the organisational pitch at the same time. That would be mass chaos – can you imagine everyone at Old Trafford all piling onto the pitch because they want to play? Not a pretty sight. But I am advocating everyone who has something to contribute, should do so in the most appropriate way. Just sitting back on the sidelines doesn't even deserve the team jersey.

Questions

● When you attend meetings or training sessions, are you there as a prisoner? A vacationer? A sophisticate? An explorer?
● Why? Is that how you would really like to be?
● What keeps you from being that?

Alzheimer's or Just Lost in Space?

In a recent issue of 'The Log' (the Journal of the British Airline Pilots Association), there is a story about CRM. Now, not being an airline pilot, I wasn't even sure what CRM stood for until I read a bit. CRM is 'crew resource management', and the article told about the training that pilots need to undergo to be able to effectively manage what goes on in the planes they fly. What intrigued me about the story were two statements; 'it may be that CRM training is less effective than we think', and, 'pilots may perform perfectly in CRM training scenarios but revert to old ways and cultural habits on the line'. Now substitute 'CRM training' for almost any business training course and if you believe, 'this sure doesn't apply to our company' then come back from the planet Neptune and face the real world.

Why is it that we (speaking collectively for the managers of the world) can send employees off to training programmes, workshops and seminars – all of which may take anywhere from one day to several weeks – and expect that when they come back, they will be 'different'? What rock have we been living under?

Here is the deal. When I was in school, I was pretty good at memorising 'stuff' for tests. When I would come home with good grades, my parents were quite happy because they were under the impression that I had 'learned' something. If you were to ask me some of the same questions that were on the tests today, I would fail miserably. And it is because I really didn't *learn* it. However, I did learn how to ride a bike, drive a car and do other things I *wanted to learn*. But the things I was told by the teacher I *had* to learn I dumped after the test because they weren't important enough for me to remember. So often, we send employees off to training with the expectation that they will *learn* something, because we aren't necessarily happy with the way they do things now. On the surface, that makes sense. Where we fail is that we forget that it is pretty difficult to *unlearn* some of the behaviours that we have acquired over many years, especially if the 'learner' is quite happy to keep doing things they way he or she is comfortable doing them. This was a point of the article in the pilot magazine.

Pilots of airlines are sent off to flight simulators to learn what to do in certain situations – like when an engine fails, or when a passenger begins to run amok in the back of the plane, or when all the trendy electronic stuff onboard (the stuff that is supposed to fly the plane) fails and they have to do the flying again. As a frequent flyer, I am quite pleased that they do this. But some of the airlines have found that in high-stress situations, some of this *new learning* fades away and the way that crews behave resembles more like how they have in the past. The same is true with managers and employees in business. The pilots knowing this stuff is important – the question is, will they remember it when they need to?

We send managers off to learn new technical and interpersonal skills. In today's business world, this is clearly necessary. But to expect that after *learning* new skills in some course, they will actually forget all the old behaviours is like believing that Mr Bin Laden will be nice if we could just have him take a course in kindness. Our ability to resolve problems has been honed over years of experience doing just that. And the way we interact with others is a product of how we have learned to do it in the past. But in many organisations I have seen, there is a real need to improve managerial skills, learn how to resolve problems differently than we have in the past, and change the way managers interact with employees. So we send managers off to some seminar, course or workshop to learn how. The question is, faced with a potential stressful situation, will they be able to use the new skill they *learned*, or will they simply do what they have always done? And even more importantly, what are some of the unintended consequences that might arise if they do revert to the old ways?

A way out of this is to have businesses provide 'practise fields' for managers to hone their new skills, to become more comfortable using them, and to enable them to replace the old skills. Sure, letting managers spend some time trying out using the new skills may take time (which means cost money), but if they are not comfortable using them, they probably will simply revert back to old behaviours when the 'stuff hits the fan'. Can we afford that today?

Learning in business is extremely important. The ability to learn faster than the competition is thought by some people to be a real differentiator in business. All fine. But do we really believe that the learning that managers need to acquire (and make stick) will really just take place over a day or so? If so, Neptune must be a pretty special planet.

Questions

- Why is it so difficult to retain and use the skills we learn?
- Do the training sessions you attend focus on teaching, or on learning?

Have We Become Just Like the Forth Bridge?

I was talking to a business leader the other day about why some management teams never seem to move forward, and she said to me, 'it sounds like the Forth Bridge'. The Forth Rail Bridge, opened in 1890 near Edinburgh, was the biggest manmade construction of its time. The bridge took seven years to build and cost a fortune. It is monumental, somewhat like some of the things businesses try to accomplish today. And like those businesses, the work on the Forth Bridge is never ending.

As the story goes, the bridge is so big, that the ongoing maintenance work on it is never ending. The painters begin on one end, and by the time they reach the other end, the end they started on needs to be repainted again. They never are able to actually 'complete' their job. The parallels to business are frightening.

Example 1: whilst sitting in on a management team meeting, I found that they were discussing an issue – an issue they had identified as critical to the success of the company – that they had been 'discussing' for the past three months. No decision about what to do to resolve the issue, just lots of discussion. This behaviour – discussing but not deciding – is a clear symptom of a management team that is not aligned, nor is willing to be held accountable for its actions. Employees can see this behaviour occur, as it will manifest itself in ways such as announced initiatives that are not funded when it comes time to deliver; mixed signals as to the priorities of the company (we say 'this' is important, but we don't do anything about it); and, potential innovative ways to deal with technology and competition that simply 'wilt' on the vine – not good signals to send.

Example 2: a rather well-known American company whose management team pushes new initiatives forward every six months or so, never allowing enough time to see the results of the initiatives to deliver sought after results. This behaviour is a classic example of management not willing to be held accountable for its actions. Managers 'show' how active they are by driving initiatives forward, but never seem to complete what they begin. But they rely on the 'beginnings' of the initiative activity to show how competent they are – a sure sign of skilled incompetence.

Example 3: a UK company whose Board keeps changing its senior management every year, creating the impression that it's reason to be in existence is to reorganise constantly, dis-allowing any ability on the part of employees to know which direction the company is going for more than several months. This is certifiable 'stirring it up' behaviour – keep everything 'up in the air' so that it appears that much is going on, but in reality, the only things that are changing are the deck chairs. This is one of the most devastating behaviours of management for it never allows employees to focus on what really needs to be done, as they spend most of their time trying to figure out who is at the helm of the corporate ship. And it is clear from history; when a new person becomes in charge, they like to 'leave their mark' on the company. Hence, directions, priorities and targets tend to change, leaving the employees and mid-managers confused and frustrated – (I don't think the editors will let me say what this results in, but it is not good).

Example 4: a pan-European company whose management team spends most of its time fire fighting instead of driving higher performance. Fire fighting – the management sport of the 21st century – is not the best thing for senior managers to be spending their time on. As a matter of fact, fire fighting anyplace in the organisation is not a good behaviour. Yes, when there is a 'fire', it must be put out; but what so many companies do is just fight the symptoms of the fire and when they seem to disappear, they are all proud of themselves for being smart guys. But because they were just attacking the symptom, the underlying problem never really goes away, resulting in it surfacing again, quite often, harsher than before. And then they 'fight it' again, and again, and again – a good example of managers who don't think systemically.

Clearly, managing a business in today's business climate is not easy. With all the technology advances that have occurred, the time that managers can 'reflect' on issues before they have to make a decision has been compressed; with the onslaught of globalisation, the ability to remain competitive and retain or grow market share has become more complex; and with unstable and volatile marketplaces, the pressure from external sources for instant success has put demands on decision makers unseen before. But aren't all those reasons that we pay our senior managers so much money? Aren't we paying them to make the tough decisions that will generate the right results? Well, I thought that was the reason. I don't think we should be paying them to exhibit behaviours as seen in the four (very typical) examples listed above.

Whilst repainting the Forth Bridge is an example of how the work really never reaches completion, management needs to become better at how they think about issues, how they influence others, how they achieve goals, and how they demonstrate real leadership. A big part of management is getting the job done. And if managers can't do that, they might as well put on some old clothes, grab a paintbrush and head up to Scotland. I hear there is a bridge there that needs constant repainting.

Questions

- Why is it so hard to finish some initiatives by the intended date, if at all?
- What can be the impact of 'non-completion' in an organisation?

Was Darwin Right?

At the risk of misquoting from *The Origin of Species*, to paraphrase Charles Darwin, 'only the strong survive'. If we accept that he was more or less right, the question might arise, 'when it comes to organisations, was Darwin right?'

Clearly, there is some logic behind the argument that only 'strong' companies are the ones that seem to be able to survive the ups and downs of the economy, of competitive threats and of the changes of customers' needs and wants. This is most often attributed to the belief that a 'strong' company has the resources to sustain itself during the slumps that inevitably occur. This belief is fine, especially if we consider 'strength' to be a function of bank balance. But is this the only 'strength' that matters for contributing to the sustainability of an organisation? The answer is no.

Organisational 'strength', whilst being supported by the depth of a company's pockets, is more importantly a function of the depth and breadth of several things; including, the ability of an organisation's people to know where the organisation is going in the future; why this direction is important; how it will get there; and the ability to make the right decision about investments to sustain the future. These variables – and they clearly are 'variable' – all impact a company's culture, the employees' motivation, and their willingness to 'go that extra mile' for the company.

A key element in becoming strong enough to be able to survive is the ability to make the right decisions about investments to sustain your company's future. Here is how this works. Your business is doing well; you have done a great job in keeping your customers happy and, in return, they keep coming back to you for more of what you do. And as their demands for additional parts, products and/or services increase, it becomes harder and harder to keep up your level of quality and on time delivery. So you invest in more and newer equipment to build your capacity.

Buying the equipment is one thing – training the employees to use it to advantage takes time and the delays can be devastating. You wish you had been able to plan for this need earlier, but you didn't so now you are behind, and your position in the market is slipping. Your customers begin to become frustrated by your inability to meet their needs because you are not producing at the levels you should. And when you finally do, your capacity is higher than the demand.

If you are lucky, the customers you have kept 'feel' your new capacity and spread the word, and your demand once again rises, and if you are like most companies, begins over time to outstrip your new capacity. Feels like being on a roller coaster, doesn't it? You cannot believe how often this happens . . . and not just to big companies or manufacturing companies. The ability to effectively balance capacity and demand is a key element in being strong enough to survive.

The problem here is two-fold. First, in most cases, when investments are made in equipment, the delay between the time of arrival and set-up and effective utilisation can be enormous. It is this delay that causes the problems, usually because the recognition that there even would be a delay is not visible. New equipment means the need for training on how to use the equipment increases. Training employees to use new equipment requires new skills, and being able to acquire and apply the new skills takes time. And during this delay, employees can become frustrated, and that can increase the delay time. Planning for the delay means understanding that there will be a delay, that the delay in employees learning new performance behaviours will take time, and that the delays can negatively impact your ability to deliver on your promises to customers.

Second, when business (and profit) begins to slip, usually one of the first things to be cut from budgets is training. And if you cut your training budgets, your ability to keep evolving your company to meet and exceed customer demands (the key to keeping your customers happy) will sink faster than the Titanic after hitting the iceberg. Training, at all levels, is one of the most often missed opportunities for companies that have a desire to be strong enough to survive. And training does not just mean teaching people to operate machines more effectively. Training also applies to senior and mid-managers who need to keep learning new ways to demonstrate leadership to employees.

Is this hard work? Will this take time away from the employees' real jobs? Well, sure it will. But the reality is that making an investment in time now can pay major benefits in the future. A workforce that doesn't have a clear picture of what you are trying to achieve will not be very effective in helping you get there. And if they can't see what you are trying to achieve, or for what reasons, or how their actions can contribute to that success, they will become disenchanted, de-motivated and, eventually, resistant to initiatives. And you will not be able to afford that, because if it happens, then your organisation will not have the strength it needs to survive.

If this happens to you, Darwin will still be right, and your organisation just won't make it to the future. Is that a risk worth taking?

Questions

- Which is believed to be better in your organisation: to be in control, or to ensure that everyone knows what to do and why to do it?
- Which one of these mental models do you hold?
- Which one is held by your management team?

The $65 Pain Reliever

Whew, did you hear it? It was the collective sigh of relief on the part of managers in the energy sector this week when the price of oil hit $65 per barrel again. And do you know why they are relieved? Think back a bit to when the price of oil was a lot lower. What was the message that we were hearing? In many corners, the message was that managers were not competent to make sound decisions, and the evidence of that was the fact that many companies in that sector were not making the profits that they were expected to make. And now it has all changed. Profits are rolling in.

The question is, 'are these companies making expected profits due to managers' decisions or is it because the price of oil has risen?' And this question then brings forth another question, 'is profitability a fair indicator of managerial ability?'

Well, I would think that many managers in the petroleum sector would say yes, but I am not sure. First, if profitability is a fair indicator of managerial competence, then should it be profitability 'every month of every year instead of once in a while when the price of oil goes up?' And how many companies are able to deliver that? Apparently, not too many. And what about companies from other sectors, such as the airline industry? As the price of oil goes up, profits for airlines will plummet as operating costs escalate. Managers in this industry would respond with, 'using profitability as an indicator of competence is not fair, as this (the price of oil) is beyond our control'. Okay, fair enough. But by the same reasoning, then if oil prices fall and help restore profits to the airlines, then these profits are beyond your control as well, aren't they?

Making effective business decisions should be a recognised competency in all business sectors, and this means regardless of external influences. Okay, sure, you might be thinking that because external influences are things that managers have no control over, they should not be held accountable for their impact. If this is what you believe, that's fine . . . but this view is a myopic one. Managers are paid (and usually paid well) to make decisions that will help their respective organisations achieve company goals. I don't know of a single company where this statement only applies to *'when things go our way'*. No, making effective decisions means making effective decisions regardless of the situation.

Part of making effective decisions means not only knowing the current situation, but looking at contingencies that may impact the current situation. Some may recognise this as scenario planning, some may recognise this as contingency planning, but I tend to think of it as just plain common sense. And for some reason, it just doesn't occur in business today as often as it should.

This could be because when things are good (when companies are showing profits), there seems to be no reason to worry about what else might happen. And when things are bad (lack of profits or profits that do not meet expectations), the main drive is to 'crank' on the business to get the profits back. The common sense part is to understand what might happen that could reduce profits *before* it occurs.

The only way that managers will be able to do this is if they begin to do things differently. And the things that they need to do differently include examining how they think about the issues their company (division/department/business unit) is facing; how they influence others to meet the challenges they face; how they achieve the goals and targets they are charged with achieving; and how they demonstrate leadership to their people. These are common sense managerial competencies. Too often, however, the only competency that is focused on is *achieving* – hitting the numbers. If the numbers are not achieved, the manager is quite often thought of as incompetent. Well, the point is that if managers don't begin to think differently, influence others differently, and demonstrate leadership differently, the ability to achieve will not change . . . and companies' profit potential will continue to be at the mercy of outside influences. And that just isn't good enough.

When many companies, from all sectors, have environments in which managers and employees suffer from malaise, low morale, low motivation and poor consistency in results, it is clear that something needs to be done differently. And what needs to be done differently is to change the thinking, influencing, achieving and leading behaviours of managers.

Will this take time and cost money? Well, of course it will – any time you make an investment, it costs money. And that is exactly what changing behaviours of managers is, an investment . . . an investment that is more powerful than any piece of equipment. This investment is more powerful because if managers begin to change their decision making behaviours based on how they think, how they influence, how they achieve and how they lead, there is a good chance that they will be able to deliver profitability to the companies they work for – regardless of some of the external influences that plague them.

And don't think that just because the price of oil went up again that managers in the energy sector are not feeling plagued by oil cost volatility, even though it has made them look good again. What goes up will come down again. Always did, always will. But that's okay; maybe some of them will use this 'up' time to come up with excuses for when it goes down.

Questions

- Does your company hit its goals and targets because of the decisions of management or because 'things just went right?'
- Who takes credit for the achievement of goals and targets?

Can We Really Do More with Less?

We know that one of the forces driving change today in business is the need to increase the effectiveness of employees. Okay, so this newsletter is supposed to be *Plain Talk about Business Performance*, so maybe I should make this point a bit clearer – the big thing today is to see how we can get more out of our employees with less. Clear enough?

There is no doubt that getting more from less is important, and in a business world where cost cutting due to whatever reason is so crucial, it is even more critical. Here are a couple of examples of what I mean.

You manage a group of people in your department and have just been given a directive that you need to reduce your budget by some fixed amount, but at the same time, are given targets that are higher than you had in the past. And, as you are not exactly new on this planet, you know what is going to probably happen. The employees who work for you (the ones who will still have their jobs after some of them are let go due to the cutbacks) are going to become highly stressed out; they will begin to fall into reactive thinking mode; they will make mistakes in the way they make decisions; and all this will lead to burn-out. And then your ability to deliver upon the 'promises' that you are expected to deliver upon will be diminished. And all of this is on top of the extra workload that you and your people have due to the last round of cutbacks.

Now, if this picture is not grim enough, think about it when it occurs in an intended team environment. You have cross-functional managers and employees working to develop collaborative solutions to long-standing problems. The good news is that both sides of the team – sometimes union and management – are very committed to shifting the game so that the company can do better (and survive). But one of the managers who is working to act as a co-chair of the team is under such pressure due to the cutbacks he has been dealing with that his ability to contribute has been diminished terribly by being stretched in so many directions – all because the company needs to get more done with less.

Okay, so to be honest here, it is a tough world out there, and there is a train of thought that says 'if the fire is too hot, then get out of the kitchen'. Cute advice that is usually proffered by those who are not under this type of pressure. And if everyone who was under this type of pressure decided that the pressure was too great and just quit, then the company would be in even deeper problems, so that is clearly not the answer.

There are a couple of ways to get through some of this, and the ones that make the most amount of sense are to make sure that your managers (or employees) who are fast approaching the point of burn-out make sure that they have a clear picture of what their priorities really are, and then equip them to manage their time appropriately.

Both of these points are critical: feeling stretched so thin that there is no way to be effective in any task will cause burn-out, and then the employee is in a fix; not being able to manage required priority time will end up with the same result. Both of these will lead to mediocre performance at best, which then leads to lack-lustre results and demoralisation.

Being able to understand what the most important priorities are (and in today's business world, everything tends to look like a priority) can only improve the potential that the efforts that are available will be put in the right places. And when you know what your priorities are, you are better able to work with others to help them see the same areas that need to be addressed. When this does not occur – when priorities are 'foggy' or confusing – there is a tendency that they will be missed. And all that does is create negative perceptions about the ability of managers (and teams) to get the job done. And consequently, it won't get done.

The best way to help sort out what the real priorities are is to determine which of them are 'urgent' and which are 'important'. Urgent issues normally are things that must be done immediately, usually because they were neglected in the past. Important issues, however, are the ones that will most effectively help the organisation achieve its goals, targets and satisfy its mission. Too often, we can get sidetracked by believing that some things that we perceive to be priorities are, in fact, just 'stuff' that really adds no value to the organisation. And it is these 'distractions' that can cripple our ability to stay focused on the issues that will improve performance and increase our ability to realise the potential of our organisations.

By enabling managers and teams to 'see' this difference, they are better able to manage their time effectively and avoid burn-out, sloppy decision making and demoralisation.

Most organisations can do more with less, but only if their managers and employees are not burned out, making mis-directed decisions or demoralised. Can this choice be any clearer?

Questions

- How are priorities decided upon in your organisation?
- How does your organisation work to prevent management and employee burn-out due to workload constraints?

Why Can Collaborative Efforts Become Adversarial?

Improving performance is all about changing behaviours. Period. So, having said that, I suppose it is only fair to now get into why changing behaviours can be so difficult. For one thing, too often, we don't even see anything wrong with our behaviours. Take the question of 'why can collaborative efforts become adversarial?'

This is a good question, and as with most good questions, there is a short answer and a long answer to it. To better understand the answers, it might be easier to look a bit closer at the question to understand what it really means. Collaborative efforts are the result of business (and non-business) environments in which there is more than one business unit and the business units are supposed to work together to get a better result. This is the whole 'synergy thing' in action; combined effective efforts bring higher gains in performance.

So here is how collaborative efforts are supposed to work. You have an organisation that has, on the surface, one or two really big goals that all business units are charged with supporting. The goals are developed as part of an overall strategy, and with the high level goals usually comes departmental goals and departmental budgets to achieve them with. When each department (or division or business unit) achieves its goals, these achievements all add together to support the achievement of the overall company goal. That is how it is supposed to work, and in most cases, it does.

But in some organisations, what actually occurs is that as each individual department puts forth their efforts to achieve its goals, they quite often end up doing activities that can be counterproductive to the efforts of other departments who are just trying to achieve their goals. When this occurs, whilst one department may achieve the gains it seeks, other departments may not be able to do the same. And the effect of this begins to ripple through the overall organisation and can be especially devastating in recently merged companies.

One of the most often seen reactions to this is a drive for additional budget funding, either to acquire additional assets, equipment or human resources. But all that does is potentially shift the achievements from one department to another, and this sets up a dynamic known as escalation – *you* have more assets than I do, enabling you to do more, so *I* want more assets so I can do more, and then *you* want more, etc. And the end result is a shift from collaborative efforts to ones that are adversarial in nature. It all falls into a competition about who can *look the best*, not how collaborative efforts can provide leverage so the overall goals can be reached – a win–win situation for you as a manager, for the company, and for your customers.

Intended collaborative efforts that become adversarial can be devastating to companies. They drain resources, they waste time, they sap morale and they result in a decline in motivation – all contributing to a reduction in performance. Collaborative efforts that do work well drive innovation, creativity, production and improve motivation and organisational climate; all improving overall the potential for increased performance.

In order to avoid intended collaborative efforts from becoming adversarial, it is important to first recognise that it can and does happen. When goals and budgets are deployed, conversations should accompany them to identify the potential risk for internal adversarial activities, along with ways to identify them *before* they occur and ways to prevent them from happening.

Additionally, it is important to make sure that the goals and accompanying budgets do not *cause* the relationship to become adversarial. This is very important to recognise – quite often, one of the unintended consequences of goal deployment is that the explicit instructions and the implicit meanings can actually *drive* adversarial thinking.

Avoiding this can be done by 'testing' the impact of the goals and budgets prior to their deployment to the various departments. Testing the impact of goals and budgets can and should be done by listening to the people who will be charged with achieving the goals with the budgets they will get. Ask them to confirm that they will be able to 'make it all happen' and if they say yes, then ask them what else might happen as they do it. '*What else might happen*' is a question about potential unintended consequences, and is something that they should be thinking about. If they respond that, 'well, there might be a problem . . .' then it is time to have a different type of conversation.

This is not to say that simply because attaining goals will be hard work that managers should be cut some slack, but I am saying that the last thing you want to have occur is to set someone up for failure that will shift their thinking into an adversarial mode. This will not help the goals be achieved and, additionally, will not help build alignment in collective thinking around success.

Do these conversations take extra effort? Well, of course they do, but the real question is, 'do you want to have the goals achieved or not?' If your answer is 'yes', then you need to do what you can to avoid the potential of adversarial thinking.

Unless you work for an organisation where you can have all the resources you need, anytime you need them, then you will be running the risk that someone else will be after the same pot of money you are after to get their job done. Don't let your team's effort to get the job done become adversarial – this will not help you as a manager; it will not help the company; and it will not help your customers.

Questions

- Are some of the managers in your organisation vying for the same company resources? How do you know?
- Do their activities to obtain the same resources often put them at odds with each other, resulting in adversarial relationships?

Are We Setting Managers Up for Failure?

Pushing for increased organisational performance is important, but of equal importance is ensuring that the organisational environment is *conducive* to ensuring that performance can be delivered. There are many organisations that, on the surface, are moving in a positive performance improvement direction. But, when exploring beneath the surface, it is possible to see that these same organisations are, in reality, preventing performance to really improve. This is because many managers are creating structures in which their people are doomed to fail. The 'set up to fail' syndrome is becoming more and more clear as we learn how to better understand the various dynamics at play in organisations through research, but more importantly, through real hands-on experience.

The 'set-up to fail' syndrome is a dynamic in which a manager assumes that he or she is responsible for creating a decision making environment in which there are winners and losers. In this type of environment there are those who succeed quite well – the winners. But anyone who does not succeed to the level at which the manager expects becomes the loser. And as we all know, being a 'loser' in an organisational system is not something that can be changed easily. Most managers believe that 'once an organisational loser, always a loser' and, consequently, that person (who has become the 'loser') becomes doomed to an environment in which success very quickly takes on the appearance of 'not good enough', or mediocrity or even worse.

The dynamic looks and acts like this. There are two employees under a manager's supervision. They both have been working for the same manager in the same department for quite some time, and when pressure to improve performance increases he looks to both employees to see how they are doing. Employee 'A' has been performing well, but not as good as employee 'B'. What does the manager do? What would you, as their manager, do? You probably would begin to supervise employee 'A' a lot more than in the past. And in the process of doing that, the 'supervision' can evolve into 'second-guessing' and then a reduction in the number of decisions that employee 'A' is even *allowed* to take.

On a departmental scale, the dynamic shows up when two different business units are competing for resources. Business unit 'Y' has been successful in the past, whilst business unit 'Z' has not been delivering the performance that it is charged with delivering. You are the budgetary decision maker who has to sort out which of these business units can receive the resources it is asking for. What do you do?

Do you reward success (business unit 'Y') with additional resources so they can continue to demonstrate success? Or do you try to understand what are some of the underlying reasons that business unit 'Z' has not been delivering expected performance? In most cases, what happens is that success is rewarded.

This is as it should be – we should always reward success, but we also need to understand why some business units are not as successful instead of propagating a structure in which success will never occur. Don't forget that managers run business units and the stigma of 'low performance' sticks like glue, and then the dynamic of winners and losers continues.

Breaking this cycle can be done, but it takes a willingness on the part of senior management to ensure that managers and other decision makers work in an environment in which they can realise their potential, and are encouraged to do so. In most cases, the set up to fail syndrome is not even intentional, so it also requires a willingness to talk about the fact that it *can* occur.

Being 'set up to fail' can result from many things: managers may be given challenges and/or goals that are not clear; they may be given goals without the needed resources to attain them; they may be unintentionally prevented from attaining goals and targets by being pushed and pulled in non-valued added directions; they may be trying to satisfy 'urgent' needs instead of being able to focus on those that are important; they may be thrust into situations in which they do not have the requisite skills or competencies. The list can go on and on.

Creating an environment in which managers can realise their potential requires that they are provided with opportunities to improve their decision making skills, ensuring that they have the resources that they will require to deliver the performance that is expected of them, and they have the ability to work collaboratively.

Setting managers up for failure is a symptom of an organisation that does not value people and their ability to contribute. It is a symptom of an organisation in which 'hitting the numbers' is deemed more important than ensuring that gains that are made can be sustained. It does a disservice to its other employees, customers and shareholders. It is a symptom of an organisation that I would not want to work for. Would you?

Questions

- Do you believe that there are some managers in your organisation who have been set up to fail?
- Why?
- What are the signals of this happening?
- What can be done to avoid this?

Making Profits or Making Excuses?

When was the last time you heard some manager give reasons why he or she didn't deliver on his or her promise? Businesses from all sectors are still plagued by the same condition – a distinct lack of ability to deliver consistent, sustainable performance results. This situation is complicated of course, and if we listen to many business leaders and analysts, we are led to believe that there are many external events that are causing this. But I think it is about time that we face the reality of the situation: businesses are not delivering sustainable performance results because of the decisions that are being made about how to achieve them. Let's look at several sectors to better understand why this is.

The energy sector is faced it seems continually with external drivers that play with the price of oil and gas. Okay, so that is a given – OPEC and OPEC abusers do play havoc with the price and, consequently, the potential return on investment for energy exploration and production. When there is a 'glut' of oil on the market, the price falls and when the demand for petroleum increases, the price escalates. One would assume that managers in the energy sector would be pretty aware of this dynamic by now, after all, it has been present since the mid-1970s when OPEC appeared. And yet, the thing we hear most often from energy companies is that they *(and their profits)* are at the mercy of 'external forces'. The automotive sector is not much different. Car companies continually use the reasoning of 'external forces' to explain why they are not able to generate consistent profits – number of new car buyers, cost of labour, price of oil, competition . . . the list goes on and on.

Here is how you can tell what is going on. When business is 'good', management traditionally take all the credit for their decisions. Why not? 'Good' business leads to profits, and that is what management is supposed to deliver. But when business is 'bad', management shifts the blame for results to external forces that caused the profit gaps. As a shareholder, I want to know that the managers charged with making profits (so I make money) are in control of their destiny, and not just really good at coming up with excuses for their inability to ensure good decisions and good outcomes. As an employee, I want to know that the people leading the company are the right ones to do it.

We are faced with a choice: either to believe the managers that profit fluctuations are not within their control, or to believe that there is some other reason for this behaviour. Before you make your choice, remember that sustainable business performance results are the most impactful driver of profits, and that business performance is a direct function of the decision making process.

Well, I don't know about you, but I am convinced that the reason for the poor record of performance is tied directly to the management systems and level of leadership capacity in the managerial ranks of business today. Here is why.

Most certainly, 'external forces' play havoc with the effective implementation of growth and profit plans. But let's get real here – aren't we paying managers to be able to make decisions in *any* environment, not just in good environments? Managers and the companies that they work for need to get focused on putting in place fundamental management systems that can ensure decisions are in alignment with strategic and tactical goals and targets; and they need to ensure that they have the ability to make decisions on both the detail complexity that they face, but also on the dynamic complexity that results in the 'problems' we hear about.

Management systems that work create an environment in which business decisions are guided by both long- and short-term goals. They set up an environment in which managers at all levels are focused on what is really important and prevents them from becoming distracted by the opportunities that confront them daily that are interesting, trendy, 'sexy' and otherwise not beneficial to helping achieve the goals and targets that they are paid to achieve. Being effective in dealing with detail complexity enables managers to be able to make decisions such as how to most effectively manage the millions of pounds/euros/dollars that are in their respective budgets, as well as how to keep their staff focused on what is important 'today'. Being effective in dealing with dynamic complexity enables managers to better understand the cause and effect relationships that they find themselves mired in as they try to implement and deploy plans. Being competent in managing dynamic complexity avoids situations in which positive, collective relationships suddenly fall into adversarial relationships accidentally, preventing the attainment of goals and targets.

Is the situation we are in today reversible, or are we just doomed to see more weeks, months and years of mediocre performance from managers who seem to be in a category known as 'skilled incompetents'?

The choice belongs to those in management who are receiving all the flack from shareholders and customers. The choice is theirs alone. But if I were them, I would think long and hard before I kept on doing business as usual. Making profits is better than making excuses.

Questions

- Do external forces drive your organisation?
- What is the impact on decision making of external forces?
- How much effort is put forth to ensure that your management team creates your corporate destiny?
- What can be done to keep external forces in perspective?

Choking on Success?

If there is one thing that can kill a business besides lack of growth, it is growth that is too fast. The article in the *Daily Telegraph* of 22 June 2004 said it all – Stelios Haji-Ioannou was quoted as saying, 'The mistake we made was we grew too rapidly'. Stelios was referring to the stories about some of the business units in his EasyGroup (EasyCar, EasyInternetCafe and the other 'Easy' ventures that he is involved with). Whilst EasyJet is a well-recognised success, the statement by the founder does beg the question, 'is sustaining growth really that easy?' Apparently not.

Companies grow because they have a solid, well-recognised brand; they have happy customers who spend money with them; they have their cost structure firmly under control; and their senior managers are able to keep their eye on the ball. When any one of these variables starts to slip, growth ceases and it sends the other variables into a tailspin. And when that happens, the potential for sustainable growth ceases. So in the case of Stelios, when he said that they 'grew too quickly' – a symptom of the real problem – it was probably a reflection on the slippage of one or more of those variables.

The EasyGroup is a classic example of what can occur from fast growth. Managers begin to believe that the success they have generated can be repeated again and again. They begin to believe that their decisions will always work out right. They begin to assume that whatever they touch will turn to gold (or shocking orange in some cases). And they begin to believe that the market will follow them.

Well, sometimes they might be right. But repeatability of success can only happen when managers make sound decisions; and to do this, they need to ensure that their thinking, influencing, achieving and leading faculties are in alignment. And too often, they are not.

To prevent this from happening to your organisation, there are several things that you can do. First, begin to believe that your previous success may not solely be because you are smart. Organisational success is complex, and just because you can 'see' success again, it doesn't mean that everyone in your organisation will 'see' the same picture in the same way you do. Spend time with your team and talk through all the complexities of what you are trying to accomplish. By 'talking it through', I don't mean you tell them that the plan is to repeat what you did previously. I mean that you and your team will need to figure out all the potential scenarios that you might encounter on your hoped for journey to repeated success. I wasn't there when EasyJet was begun, but do you believe that some of the scenarios the senior team talked about included the current price of fuel to run the planes? Do you believe that they talked about the potential for a 9–11 happening and air travel falling? Do you believe that they talked about everybody and his brother getting into the discount airline business? Wasn't there, don't know. But I do know that the only way to be ready for any contingency that can muck up your plans is to know what 'might happen'. And when you know what 'might happen', you can then either build a contingency plan for it, or chuck the whole idea for being too risky.

The next thing you can do is work to avoid getting ahead of yourself. When things are going well, we quite often begin to skip over decisions that can, over time, have a tremendous impact in the future. Things worth doing at all are worth doing well. Take your time. Be sure that you have crossed all your T's and dotted all your I's. The devil is in the detail, and just rushing ahead at speed can cause some decisions to be fraught with problems.

Make sure that you have the right team of people working with you. In many organisations, the team that is charged with plotting out the future comprises like-minded people. Well, okay, you do need to have people who share the same vision. But at the same time, you need to ensure that you have a blend of people who are not afraid to raise the tough questions and to say 'no' if they think something will not work out the way you want it to. You might want to use some tool like Meyers-Briggs or OPQ or Belbin to get a grasp on what your team can bring to the decision making process. Remember, the chances of success are severely lessened if people who are all intuitive thinkers or data-heads surround you. Success in decision making comes through a blend of thinking and influencing types. A caution here of course – these tools are just that: tools. In order to really get something from them, you need to realise that they represent decision making models and their use is just a way to surface insights into why we think and react the way we do. And your team needs to realise that as well and not treat them as a cute exercise that will be over in a couple of hours.

Will Stelios be able to revisit the success he has seen in the past? Well, time will tell. But in the words of Mr Einstein, the same kind of thinking that got us into a mess will not get us out of it. Regardless of how successful you have been in the past, you need to remember that repeatable, sustainable success just isn't that easy.

Questions

- Do your managers believe that the success they have seen in the past can be sustained in the future?
- Do they believe that, because they 'did it before', they can do it again?
- What behaviours do they demonstrate to ensure that this can occur?
- What do they do to ensure that the employees have the necessary skills and resources to make this happen?

And This Week's Winner Is . . .

This is getting to be like the big BAFTA or Oscar nights – we all know who the players are, and we have a good idea who might be in contention, but sometimes we are surprised by which organisation will unleash the shock of the week. And as if this game wasn't difficult enough, even the stable, long-standing reputable companies are candidates. Sure the Enron's of the world might not have been real shockers – after all, they weren't exactly in the same league as Shell. But then Shell even became part of the game.

So, let's look back a bit. Shell announces that their reserve estimates *might be* a bit off. Then a second announcement that even the first announcement was probably wrong. Then came the finger pointing and blaming – a traditional occurrence when things go bad. And the latest – and this is also typical – is that the stories coming out of the Hague are that communications were so bad within Shell that when the 'bad' news began to come out, there was no way to verify much of anything. Clearly, there is something going on in the management of Shell that could lead one to think that the big problems that Shell is facing are not the missed reserve estimates. Shell is undoubtedly suffering from malaise or skilled incompetence. Or probably both.

Malaise is a condition where managers become way too comfortable in their jobs. They take things for granted – like performance, competence and decision making. They begin to believe that their view is 'the' view. And they begin to assume that everything will be okay – because it has always been okay. After all, if there is a problem, 'someone' will take care of it.

Skilled incompetence is a malady that shows up through decision making. It was sound decisions that helped Shell get through all the tough years, going back as far as the formation of OPEC, when Shell was one of the few players in the energy field who had developed contingency plans in case the oil prices would soar, as they did in the early 1970s. But clearly, the decision making ability at Shell had become a victim of 'why change'? Bear in mind, these are not stupid people; perhaps they just subliminally assumed that their 'smartness' would get them through anything. And Shell is not the only company today that is suffering from managerial malaise and skilled incompetence. The question should be, 'how to stop it'?

There are two things that need to be done when an organisation is demonstrating either malaise or skilled incompetence. Firstly, demand higher competencies from managers, and secondly, demand internal communications become more effective. But herein lies the rub – in most organisations, when you demand higher competencies what happens is that managers are sent to school to take a week-long course in analysing 'managerialism' or some other pretty useless thing that a university has slammed together to sell to business. Managers need higher competencies in how they think about issues, how they influence others, how they achieve goals and how they demonstrate leadership. Sure these competencies are not rocket science, but the problems aren't rocket science either. Remember, the problems that surfaced at Shell had nothing to do with how to extract more oil from the seabed – they were all about how they thought about the issues, how they influenced others, how they achieved goals and how they demonstrated leadership. These are all decision making competencies, plain and simple.

And when you demand more effective internal communications from managers, what do they typically do? You've seen it – they have someone send out more useless emails, write *another* newsletter or put more mindless information on an intranet that hardly anyone reads to begin with. More effective does not mean more. More effective means getting the right information to the right people so they can make more informed decisions. But instead companies tend to just do more and more and more, and the effectiveness of decision making becomes less and less and less.

Remember how I said earlier that Shell is not the only company suffering from malaise and skilled incompetence? Well, you should love this: there is a UK-based company that is as solid as they come – or so they appear. But they too are suffering from malaise and skilled incompetence. I know this from managers whom I speak with on a regular basis. And – this is the best part – the most senior management is well aware of the problem. So guess what they have decided to do? They have decided to put together an internal working group to 'attack the problems'. No, not revenue generation problems, not sales problems, not even competitor problems – the problems of malaise and skilled incompetence. Now isn't that special – the same good old boys who have gotten the company into the problem are being charged with fixing it. This is almost like a script for *The Office*. How much progress do you think they will make? My bet is lots of activity and glowing reports (probably in multi-colour PowerPoint presentations), but nothing will change.

Companies who suffer from malaise and skilled incompetence will continue to do so until someone decides that they have had enough, and they aren't going to take it anymore. Note: 'someone' is spelled SHAREHOLDERS.

Questions

- Does your organisation suffer from skilled incompetence?
- Why is this allowed to continue?
- What can be done to stop it?
- Do your own mental models contribute to it?

Why Is 'Getting It Right' So Difficult?

Last autumn, I had been asked to sit in on the senior management meeting of an organisation that manufactures some pretty clever high-tech telecommunications devices. Whilst they have done well in the past, they were suffering – and the reason was the same reason that most manufacturing companies suffer.

When the meeting began, the managing director gave an overview of where the company was this year, and his message was not too soothing. Lots of despair; lots of finger pointing; lots of recriminations; lots of silence in the room. I couldn't resist the opportunity, so I asked the MD exactly what the problem was. His response was typical, 'the problem is that we can't get our products to market'. This sounded like a symptom of the real problem, so I said, 'Yes, I understand you aren't getting products to market, but what is the underlying problem?' 'The problem is that we don't have the number of people or the financial resources of our competitors,' he said.

Okay, so now were getting someplace, but something didn't add up. Several years previously, the company had done considerably better so I decided to push a bit for clarification. 'Several years ago, when you had better sales, did you have more people and more resources?' The room full of highly paid senior managers became even more quiet, largely because everyone there knew that when they had better sales earlier, they had even fewer people and fewer financial resources than they had now. Clearly, something else was wrong. And it wasn't until after the meeting that things began to become clear.

The managers in the meeting represented all the main functions of a company that produces the latest in technology – human resources, finance, research, design, technological innovation, production, etc. When the 'formal' meeting was over, 'real meetings' began. The concept of the 'meeting after the meeting' is very typical on management teams. Issues are talked about at the 'formal' meeting, but some of the biggest decisions are made at the 'meeting after the meeting', usually conducted with either massive lobbying or lack of dissenting viewpoints. Isn't decision making fun?

At one of these 'meetings after the meeting', two interesting things surfaced. The first was that the meeting that just had occurred was one of only three that had taken place in the previous year with all the members of the 'management team' present. The second was that in the previous three months, the guys from innovation had been able to deliver a few pretty spectacular new developments for their efforts. Now in the case of a company whose reputation rests on both the latest in technology and quality, innovation is a good thing. And even more good news came from the production guys. They had been able to re-design their production processes to make the products faster and cheaper. Okay, so let's figure this out . . . product will be more impressive than the competition and production will be able to crunch out more than ever; but the overall performance delivery didn't improve. In fact, the ability to place product into the marketplace sank faster than the Titanic after it hit the iceberg.

The fundamental problem was that the innovation guys and the production guys weren't talking to each other. They each knew that the other was working on improvements to their part of the product process, but they didn't share what the impact of those improvements might be on the rest of the company. And at the management meetings (which they all didn't bother to attend), nobody said much of anything. No wonder that the individual improvements didn't work together – no one knew what the others were doing.

Here you had an organisation producing a complex product, with all the various departments working their tails off to do what they do better. But because they didn't talk to each other, the fruits of their efforts were not necessarily helpful overall. What had happened was that, whilst the innovation guys were focused on coming up with a better product, their improvements required changes in the production process. And at the same time, the production team was doing the same thing – working their tails off to make the product faster and cheaper, which they did. But the interrelationship between the new innovations and the ability to cheaply and quickly produce a quality product didn't go together well. The new innovations meant that the new production processes would barely work at all, and resulted in massive shipping delays, which meant reduced products on shelves. No products, no sales; and no sales, no profits.

What was happening in this example is not unique. Companies from all sectors suffer from the same malady – an inability (or unwillingness) to communicate effectively in order to ensure that departmental efforts do not become counter-productive, or even worse, adversarial. All of this can happen quite innocently. When the goal of 'continuously improving' is deployed downward, the efforts tend to become 'segmented' – each unit of the business is supposed to improve what they do, with the intent being the overall product or service is better. Keeping close contact with individual improvement efforts is key to avoiding the problems that this company was having – hot innovation is great, but if it causes other design challenges that no one knows about, it is pretty hard to see how they will see the light of day.

Your company may not be involved in producing the latest in technology, but the same dynamics apply – if there is little or no communication between the company's various functions, improvements (which is what the functions are supposed to continually come up with) may not deliver their promise. And then the company and its management can't deliver its promise to shareholders either. And then there is no way you will ever 'get it right'.

Questions

- Do the managers in your organisation really understand the difference between problem symptoms and the fundamental problems that drive them?
- Which do they tend to focus their efforts on?
- Why?

Do Matrix Organisations Work?

Well, this one may get some of our readers pretty wound up, but here goes anyway. I was visiting the offices of a good-sized company a while ago and as I was being ushered into the senior VP's office, I noticed that the entire outer office area had been changed. So I asked the secretary what was going on, and she said, 'oh, the office? We do that every two years. You can set your diary by it. When we had cubicles, we change to open plan; then we change back to cubicles, then to open. We have done it since they invented the cubicle I think.' 'But why?' I asked. 'It is supposed to improve our productivity they say, but we all know that it is because every couple of years, we hire a new person who wants to leave his mark on the company.' Nice. So what is really going on here? Last week I received a phone call from a client who wanted to know what I thought about his company changing to a matrix management system. 'But why?' I asked. 'We think it will improve our productivity.' Changing from open plan offices to cubicle will not improve productivity any more than shifting from a hierarchical management system to a matrix system will. And the reason is that the logic behind these shifts is flawed.

Yes, every company should always be looking at ways to improve performance, i.e. productivity of employees. But looking solely at things like office arrangements and managerial responsibility lines won't do squat unless the managers and employees understand why they are there. This is a very important point – too often, managers and other employees believe that they are 'there' to do a specific set of job tasks. The 'secretary' provides support functions for his or her boss; the manager 'manages' people or processes or systems. But these views are rather myopic and result in less than optimal performance. Let's go straight to the matrix example to see why.

Here was a company that had been in business for quite a few years, and although they never really had achieved superior performance, they were doing pretty well. And then a new senior manager was brought in and he wanted to 'make his mark' on the company. To do that, he decided to change the reporting structure of all the managers, and guess why? He had read some articles about matrix management and thought that the examples in the articles made sense (which they probably did), so he decided to give it a go. They hired some matrix management 'experts' (where do these people come from, anyway?) who came up with the 'right' matrix responsibilities, and then they rolled the big plan out. Here is a rough chronology of what happened next: the 'announcement' of the change in reporting structures was made; people became confused; performance slipped due to the confusion; lots of gaming the system ensued; performance slipped further; people were 'cranked on' to 'get with the programme', motivation declined, performance slipped further . . . do you want me to go on?

What the company had done was spend some time telling all the employees who would be affected by this change what was going to happen, why it was going to happen, and how their reporting structures would be from that day on. What they had failed to do was spend some time helping the employees see their own mental models about how they view the company, its goals, its mission, and its ability to be viable over time; as well as how they view what it takes to consistently deliver high performance, individually and collectively. Without these conversations, one reporting structure or another will not necessarily improve performance.

Now I realise that some readers will probably be saying right now that this is all just a bunch of soft-skill hooey. Well, if that is what you think, then that is what you think. But also think about this: there is no 'right way' to do anything in business — there are only ways that are better than others, and even these are highly situational. A straight-line hierarchical structure may be the best, just as a matrix structure might be the best; but neither one of them is 'right'. And the idea that just changing the reporting structure will 'automatically' result in higher performance is about as daft as believing that the lottery ticket you bought last night is a sure winner.

Changing reporting structures (or for that matter, changing just about anything) in business for the sake of changing them is foolish . . . no, it is just plain dumb. Business decision makers need to only change things that don't work, but first, they need to understand why they don't work. And in business, the basic reason that companies are not able to consistently deliver high performance is because the managers and employees have different mental models about what is important, how they fit in the organisation, and how to do what needs to be done.

Do matrix organisational structures work? Of course they do. Any organisational structure can work — you just need to make sure that everyone sees the same picture of why and how and how they fit into that picture.

Questions

- Does your current organisational structure function effectively?
- Does it work as well as it could?
- Is the structure aligned with the goals of the company?
- Are the goals in alignment with the structure?

Achieving Checklist

1 How do you know what the organisation needs you to accomplish?
2 How are these goals communicated to you?
3 Are you able to see the connection between your efforts and the overall organisation goal achievement?
4 When you are given goals to achieve, are you given access to the appropriate level of resources that will be needed?
5 How do you know that what you have been asked to do is the best thing? In the best way?
6 Are you given latitude in how you will accomplish your goals?
7 How much feedback are you encouraged to provide regarding goals and methods to achieve them?
8 Are you a member or leader of a team? Do the other members really perceive the group to function as a team, or simply a group of people who are given a challenge?
9 When implementing organisational initiatives, how much effort is put forth to explore what unintended consequences might occur?
10 Do you believe that when given a goal to achieve, you need to do the work yourself, or do you believe that you should just ensure that it gets done? Why do you believe what you do?

04

Leading

Whilst all four themes of this book are extremely important, I find it hard to believe that 'leading' doesn't carry some special importance. This is where we see the big difference between management and leadership – and they are two different ways to get the job done. Managing is all about keeping things under control; leading is all about creating an environment in which things are done because people know they should get done.

Managers and employees follow both people who demonstrate hard-core management, as well as hard-core leadership. The difference is that they follow 'managers' because managers have control and power. They follow leaders because leaders are people who inspire, motivate and energise employees to realise their personal and collective potential.

Think of some of the people you know, or have heard about, who are (or were) great leaders. What made them different? What did they do to inspire people? What have they done to motivate people?

I know many senior management types and find it interesting that the majority of them believe that leadership is the way forward but, in many cases, believe that being a 'manager', i.e. managing employees, is what is needed to achieve the goals of the organisation. Think about some people who have been faced with virtually insurmountable goals for a population group. Did they succeed through 'driving' the people, or did they succeed because they inspired and motivated the people to achieve the impossible? In most cases, the path chosen was one of leadership.

Being a leader can seem to be hard. It requires a level of understanding of what needs to be accomplished, and why. It requires a clear understanding of what skills are needed, and in which areas. It requires high levels of thinking and influencing competencies. And it requires patience. But taking the path of leadership is the easiest way to accomplish what needs to be accomplished in an organisation. Without clear leadership, most organisations resort to using hard-core management to drive initiatives and to do this – to ensure that things do get done, on time and in full – requires organisational 'policemen' to keep the pressure on. This is both costly (additional staff who really add no value to what an organisation does) and not sustainable (soon you will need policemen to police the existing policemen). Not an inspiring future. Not a motivating future. And not a future that can help people to realise their potential.

Because I believe that leading is far more powerful than managing (and clearly different), I have chosen a series of stories that outline the leverage provided by the clear demonstration of leadership in an organisation. Regardless of sector, regardless of size, regardless of anything . . . leadership is perhaps the single biggest leverage to achieving high performance that is sustainable over time. If the people at the top of an organisation are able to demonstrate leadership, you will find that managers do think differently, they influence others appropriately, and they do achieve goals in the most effective way. It is, at the end of the day, all about leadership. These stories show why and how to become a leader.

The Summer Solstice – Longest Day or Day of Reckoning?

A few weeks ago we experienced the summer solstice – you know, the longest day of the year in the Northern Hemisphere. And I thought this might be a good time to do a little re-cap of where business has found itself. But as I was about to write, I first decided to look up what the summer solstice really is all about. According to a web-site definition, '*Falling on or about June 22nd, the Summer Solstice is a time of light and of fire. It is a time to reflect upon the growth of the season: the seeds that were planted in the earth and the seeds planted in our souls. It is a time of cleansing and renewal*'.

Okay, fine. So we did see that actual date come and go, and according to the past six months business news, it sure has been a time of light and fire for some companies and their leaders. And the growth thing? Well, outside of a few exceptions, this hasn't been the best time for seeing company growth unless, of course, you believe that the only way to grow is through acquisition. And then you would think it was a bumper crop. And if you ask me, it most certainly is a time for cleansing and renewal – the cleansing of managerial behaviours that demonstrate that so many senior people out there still just don't get it.

Whilst there is mass confusion about whether business failures are up or down, there does seem to be agreement on the fact that most businesses are not realising their potential. And there is a good reason for that – many business 'leaders' don't seem to have a clue what their respective organisational potentials even are. Goals and targets are set, in many cases, with a 'stretch' in mind. That is fine, but unfortunately, the way it works in human nature is that when a goal or target is approaching, many managers begin to 'slow down' a bit – after all, they are quite confident that their charge of meeting specific performance targets will be met, so why put forth any additional effort? And what do you suppose occurs then? Do they then begin to help managers in their organisations who are struggling to hit their own goals? Do they share excess resources with others? No, of course not. And why not? Because the reward and compensation structures that are in most organisations do not support that. Instead, managers tend to work to 'lock-in' their budgetary requests for the subsequent year and/or begin to shuffle performance into the next year in order to ensure that they repeat their 'great' performance. Can this be good for business? Can it be good to keep managers focused solely on their own 'piece of the corporate pie' and not on the overall picture? I don't think so.

And can organisations in today's business climate continue to be run by people who, by most counts, are considered to be good managers but not the best leaders? Can we continue to have organisations that are headed up by (well-paid) people who are not willing to be held accountable for the results that their companies are delivering? Can we continue to have organisations in which the most often used phrases are, 'I didn't know about that', and 'well, it isn't my fault'. I don't think so.

Perhaps we do need to think of the summer solstice of 2005 as the day in which we all revise our mindsets of what acceptable behaviour is in business. Perhaps we need to be willing to stand up and say that ethical business behaviour – at all levels – is the only behaviour that we are willing to accept. Perhaps we need to commit to helping our collective organisations realise their potential, instead of just pounding away at some semi-mythical set of goals and targets that external people say are important.

Questions

- Do the managers in your organisation recognise that they and their decisions are part of a bigger picture?
- Do they achieve through leadership or management?
- Would they change if they could?

Is There More Going on Than Meets the Eye?

You bet there is. Whenever I am asked to take a look at some new initiative or a plan for a client, it is the first thing I think of. There is a good reason for this. When managers put together a plan to do something, they tend to focus on their obvious objective: increase productivity, or drive market share gains, or improve profits, or whatever. Well, on the surface that all makes sense. But quite often, in their zeal to 'hit the numbers they have been told to hit', they can become distracted from seeing some of the unintended consequences of the plan.

This is because what is usually shown as a plan or an initiative tends to only look at the 'surface' issues that are of concern – the numbers. Rarely do they dig deeper to talk about the 'what else might happen when we roll it out'. It is the 'why' and the 'what else' that should carry as much concern as the 'what to do' and 'how to do it'.

When attempting to look deeper into a plan or initiative, there are several 'rules' to remember. These 'rules' can dictate if the plan or initiative will go as hoped for. They include:

Cause and effect are not closely related in time and space. We all understand cause and effect – if you touch a hot stove, you will get burned – the immediate impact (effect) of a cause. But when considering organisational decisions, the effects can be numerous and 'seem' semi-removed from the decision itself. And quite often, the effects of the decisions are not visible until after a delay – in many cases, a considerable delay. Think of not only what will happen initially from the decision, but why may happen six months or a year later, *after* the plan or initiative has been rolled out. Your plan is what you believe will happen; think of what 'else' will happen besides what you want to happen.

The easy way out leads back in. In most organisations, there is a big push to take immediate action when faced with a problem. This is classic quick-fix, fire-fighting thinking – when a fire is raging, put it out. Good, logical thinking. But, unfortunately, in most cases, putting the fire out only deals with the symptom of the fire, and not the underlying, fundamental cause of the fire. And consequently, after a delay, the fire comes back once again. By taking the easy way out of a problem, we tend to find ourselves back in the same situation again. When looking for solutions, think about what you are addressing – the problem, or just the symptom of the problem. And then think of what some of the unintended consequences of quick-fix thinking might be.

Behaviours will get worse before they get better. Whenever an organisational population is faced with a change in the way that they do business, their ability to continue their level of productivity is diminished. After a 'learning curve', the desired performance level should be attained, and usually is. That is the plan.

However, the depth and breadth of the slump in productivity are controlled by the ability of the population to learn and apply that learning. Be prepared for a dip in performance when you plan your initiative – and remember, performance does not only mean financial performance. Performance can mean motivation, innovation or organisational climate, and all of these can dip when you try to roll out the new initiative. Don't give up just because you see the performance drop initially. The hardest part of learning something new is being able to 'unlearn' some of what you already know. Have an environment in which the employees can learn new ways to perform better, unlearn some of the old ways, and then be able to make a real difference in their performance.

There are no right answers. This 'rule' seems to go against any good consulting methodology, but it is the semantics that are critical here. By definition, if there is a 'right' answer to a question, then every other answer must be 'wrong'. Decision making is not like mathematics where you can prove there is a 'right answer'. In organisational decision making, there are answers to questions that are most certainly better than others, but that does not make them 'right'. Being right is a situational thing – what is right today, may not appear to be right tomorrow. Make sure you don't fall into the trap of thinking that what you are about to do is the only option you have. Think about what other options you have . . . and then think harder.

Structure drives behaviour. Structure includes the explicit and implicit policies and procedures that cause organisational employees to act in one-way or another. Structures also include the messages of stated company or departmental goals. Structures are what people are actually able to accomplish. They are the physical layout of a process or a facility. And they are the mental models that the employees of an organisation have regarding their beliefs and assumptions of how the organisation should get the work done. And to make things even more complicated, it is not just the structures that drive behaviours; it is the way they are communicated.

Rolling out a new plan or initiative can be full of the excitement of a challenge and the anticipation of a better way to do something. But it can also be a time in which a company finds itself at a fork in the road. Knowing which fork to take can be a lot easier if, prior to implementing the decision, you consider these 'rules'. There *is* more going on than meets the eye, and these 'rules' can help you find it.

Questions

- Are these 'rules' or the concepts behind them talked about at the management level of your organisation?
- What prevents managers from following them?
- What would it take to ensure a clear understanding of them?
- How could these 'rules' be used in the decision making process in your organisation?

Well, I Know the Answer, but What was the Question Again?

A friend just reminded me of a book from the mid-1990s titled *A Hitch-hikers Guide to the Galaxy*. The book was about a point in time when a race of super intelligent beings built a computer named Deep Thought. It was commissioned to solve the ultimate question – you know: life, the universe, everything. The program ran for several million years and the technicians around when it finally spewed out the ultimate answer ('42') were more than just a bit confused. 'The real problem,' said Deep Thought, 'is that although 42 is definitely the answer, you don't really know what the question was.'

Is this happening to some of our decision makers today? Are we losing the plot about what we are trying to accomplish in business?

Business exists to make money. Yes, the mission statements are full of nice words about doing good and all, but the bottom line is that businesses are supposed to make money. But this is where the confusion might be coming in. Does 'make money' mean just 'make money this quarter'? Does 'make money' mean 'just make money this quarter at the expense of the next quarter'? Or, does 'make money' mean that the company is supposed to consistently make money, regardless of other conditions? I would like to think that the issue is the latter. But if this is the case, then it brings us to another question.

How are we supposed to be able to make money consistently – regardless of other conditions – when the world economy is so volatile; when competition is so powerful; when regulatory bodies come up with conditions that we have to operate under; when external analysts are telling you how well you should be doing, when . . . well, you get the point. There is an answer out there, and it is not 42.

The answer is to make better decisions. This is what managers get paid for in business. Actually, this is what managers get paid to do in any organisation, whether it is government, higher education, not-for-profits or service organisations. They get paid to make decisions that will enable their respective organisations to realise their potential. And not just for the next quarter.

Making sound decisions is usually not rocket science. As a matter of fact, making sound decisions is usually just a matter of common sense. It is much like thinking in terms of your company being on a journey. You are at a point I will call 'X' and you are trying to get to a point I will call 'Z'. The common sense path from X to Z is pretty clear – 'X' to 'Y' to 'Z'. Okay, so maybe along the way you may encounter more than one 'Y', but at the end of the day, the common sense path is 'X' to 'Y' to 'Z'. Where we lose track is in the realisation that sometimes this path is not a straight line. And we can become even more confused when one of the 'Y's that we encounter along the way is so far off the straight-line path that we lose sight of where 'Z' even is. If we are really serious about our managers making the best decisions possible to keep our organisations on path, we need to equip them with several things.

First, managers need to have a clear picture of where their organisation (or their part of the organisation) is to begin with. They need to know what the current reality is, both in terms of traditional measurements like budgets and resources, but also in terms of alignment and commitment on the part of their employees. Next, they need to have an equally clear picture of what the expectations are that they are supposed to deliver upon. They need to know that they are both responsible and accountable for delivering on these expectations. And that they will not be put in a situation in which success is unobtainable.

Managers need to have access to the data they need to make sound decisions. They need to have the ability to create (or recreate) systems and processes that will enable them to do what they are charged with doing. And – this could be one of the most important things – they need to be able to demonstrate to their employees that they believe in what they are doing; and they believe in the willingness of their employees to do the same.

I don't know of very many successful decision makers today who really believe that they have all the answers. Oh sure, I know quite a few who *profess* to have all the answers – after all, that is why they were given the jobs as key decision makers. Because someone thought they had the answers. But the reality is that it is almost impossible to have all the answers today. Being willing to stand up in front of your team and say, 'I may not have all the answers, but I know that if we work together with some common sense, we can accomplish whatever we choose to accomplish' is a very powerful signal to a team. It says that you value their input and that you want to work with them. And it says that whilst you may be 'the' manager, you are all in this together. And with an environment like that, it means that regardless of conditions, you will probably be able to make money consistently. Which is, as I recall, what business is all about.

Knowing the answers in business is important. But knowing what the questions can be is even more important.

Questions

- Has your senior management team presented a clear picture of where the organisation is going?
- Does this picture contain metrics of progress other than just financial ones?
- Is your management team equipped to keep the organisation on track?
- Will the management team be able to deal with situations that arise that may take the organisation off the planned path?

Are You on the 'Peter the Great'?

In mid–2004 I heard a story on the BBC that said that the Peter the Great, the largest nuclear warship of the Russian navy, was being immediately recalled to Murmansk for urgent repairs. The reason was that several days earlier, naval inspectors had been on board and discovered that 'where the Admirals walked and lived, everything was in good condition, but where they didn't go, the ship was in dire condition and there was a great risk that the problems could destroy the ship itself. And the Admirals were not aware of the problems'. So is this a metaphor for some of what has been happening in business or what?

Think about what the story that was reported says – not just the words on the surface, but what is behind those words. 'Where the Admirals walked and lived, everything was good.' Well, naturally, the Admirals are the 'senior management' of the organisation, and we know that things are usually nice for them. But according to the inspector's report, where the Admirals didn't go, 'the ship was in dire condition . . . and the Admirals were not aware of the problems'.

So, think about some of the organisations you know about. Does the senior management team *really know* what is going on in the company? Are they really in-tune with what it is like to do the real work of the company? Are they aware of the culture of the company and its impact on the company's ability to deliver high performance? Or have they been kept in the dark for some reason?

In most cases, they don't know, but not because they don't want to know. They don't know because so many people are afraid to deliver 'bad news' to senior managers.

First, let's take a look at the whole subject of what bad news even is. I have always thought that there are only two types of news – good news and bad news. Good news is what it says it is – information about success, information about performance increases, information about increasing market share increases, etc. Of course, this is all good news. And it should be. Bad news is usually thought of as the opposite. But the reality is that the only 'bad news' is *not knowing what is going on*. Not knowing is horrendous news, because if you don't know, there is no way you can do something about a problem until it is too late.

So, if you accept my definitions of good and bad news, then a worthwhile question to explore might be why are we hesitant to talk about news that is less than exciting? And why do some of us think that *not telling the bosses* will be better than letting them know what is really going on?

Think of what happens when you 'don't know' and then get the 'big surprise'? First, a lot of yelling and screaming goes on – which is not really helpful, nor does it create the environment in which someone would even want to bring you less than good news. Second, reactive thinking tends to kick in – you know, the 'something has to be done right now' thinking. Whilst reactive thinking may seem to be better than no thinking at all, it does tend to just deal with the symptoms of the problems, and not the problems themselves. And third, the really big one in the list of 'what happens when you finally find out', is that quite often, as we have seen in the media, there is an effort put forth to somehow disguise the bad news so it doesn't look so bad. As if that will change anything. These behaviours only reinforce the belief that 'bad news' is bad and should not be brought to the attention of your superiors. And that, my friends, is a recipe for disaster.

There is a solution, and it is that business leaders need to make it perfectly clear that they would rather know what is *really* going on, than *not know* what is really going on.

Make part of meeting agendas a forum to discuss what is really going on in your company. Get out of the office and see what is really going on. Sit with your employees at coffee breaks and ask them how things are going, ask them what they know that you don't know. Usually, it is the front line employees who are the ones who 'really know', and in most cases, they will take the opportunity to tell you. But you will have to ask, and to do that, you have to talk with them.

Don't just rely on the information from your direct reports; after all, they are probably the ones who have the greatest fear of telling you what is really going on. But also realise; if your direct reports do have a level of fear of giving you 'bad news', it is probably because you have created an environment in which that fear has become real. Tell them that you *want to know* 'all' the news, regardless if they think it is good or bad.

If our organisations are to become more effective in consistently delivering high performance, managers need to improve the way in which they make decisions. And to do that, they need to have feedback on their previous decisions, and sometimes this might mean that they get feedback that is not especially good. The alternative is to make decisions in some fairyland environment in which we think that everything is good. Well, get over it. Knowing both the 'good and the bad' news is better than not knowing. Unless you want a job as one of the Admirals on the Peter the Great . . . assuming it makes it back to Murmansk in one piece.

Questions

- Do the senior managers in your organisation know what is going on in the front lines?
- Is it considered 'safe' in your organisation to bring 'bad news' to the senior management?
- What happens when you do?
- How could you help ensure that senior management wants to know what is going on, regardless if they perceive it to be good or bad news?

Marie Antoinette Must be Alive and Well . . .

Does the term 'let them eat cake' ring a bell with anyone out there? It was reported recently that the Chairman of Telewest has been awarded a deal worth £3.4m and over a million share options – all at a time when the company's current restructuring efforts will devastate former shareholders. The actual deal seems a bit complex, but the bottom line is that he will receive a salary increase, a sign-on bonus, massive stock options and share options. Of course, the company was quick to report that the shares and options only vest if the company hits certain performance goals – which appear to be unspecified. And (you will love this bit . . .), if the company is taken over, all these little perks kick in. How nice for him, especially for the assumption that due to the situation the company is in, a take-over is almost a certainty.

Now, on the other hand, if you were a shareholder, you are, to put it very politely, not treated as well. Because of the restructuring effort, the company was listed on NASDAQ on the 19th with an expected price of over $13.00. Unfortunately, shareholders of the old London-listed stock will find themselves with stock converted to a value of about $.02 per share. Let's see – this is just a math question: which is more? $13.00 or $.02? Hmmmm. And which stock will the Chairman receive? Oh my goodness; the $13.00 NASDAQ stock. Who would have guessed that?

Then there is the story of Wm. Morrison, England's fifth largest supermarket chain, with an annual turnover of £3.9 billion. According to media reports, the Chairman of the company has been quite open about his desire to cut costs after the acquisition of Safeway last year. Makes sense – no reason to have overlapping systems and procedures that take away from the bottom line, does it? But in this case, just getting rid of overlapping systems and procedures was not enough. It seems that Safeway had a long-standing programme of rewarding employees who for many years had been doing their part to keep Safeway viable. The programme was one in which the employees who had put in at least ten years with the company would, when they retire, receive a 10 per cent discount card on purchases from their past employer. And what did the chairman do? He axed the pensioners' discount card as 'no longer appropriate'. Nice. Not sure how this will impact him, as he is reported to have an 'estimated £175,000 pension from the company on top of his £548,000 salary'. So no worries for him I would assume.

And the Chief Executive of Sainsbury's was in the news too. He was recently allocated 'free shares worth up to £504,000 as the company confirmed plans to scrap the staff's annual Christmas bonus'. If that wasn't enough good news for the senior 'team', the chairman of the company was granted a share bonus in excess of £2m, even though the company saw a decline in profits of 8.5 per cent in the past year. The annual Christmas bonus will be replaced by an increased staff discount. That means that the employees – over 50,000 employees who just lost their Christmas bonus – will be able to *spend more* at the company so they can enjoy some of the appreciation of senior management. Hello? Earth calling management . . . anyone home?

I realise that some decision makers may not be endowed with the same mental powers of Stephen Hawking, but come on people; I am sure we all realise that when a company's profits are down – as in the example above – some cost savings should be attempted. But in a situation where employees are 'penalised' by changing their Christmas bonuses to a plan in which the employees need to spend more money to receive a company benefit, whilst at the same time, the new CEO receives a benefit of over £500,000, it does make one wonder, 'what was in the heads of the people who made these decisions?' One can only conclude that they really didn't take into consideration any impact on the culture of the company.

And that takes us to British Airways. The story about BA concerned an employee of the company who had gone off on notion of the CIO reporting to the CEO. It is also worth noting that any newly designed organisation chart should never be deemed to be permanent. It may be prudent and rational to have an interim structure while the focus is critical and revert to the original structure once the task is done. Regardless of the decision about reporting structures, it is imperative that these decisions be transparent so that the employees do not perceive that management is just 'guessing' at what structure to have. The perception that you 'don't know' will quickly lead to a demoralised workforce that believes you are not the right people to lead the company out of the mess it is in.

As the person responsible for delivering the turnaround in performance, you will need to realise that you only have one commitment, and that is to make the turnaround effort work. Do not promise too much to managers other than the fact that the effort will be hard work, but well worth it over time. This is especially true for those who are key to the execution of some important projects connected to the overall effort. An interim organisational structure might be the best way to move forward, but ensure that those in interim jobs realise that the positions are only temporary and are a vehicle to achieve stability in the company. This is not to say that interim positions are not marvellous opportunities for managers to 'prove themselves' through the demonstration of high performance; this just means that temporary positions should not send the message that they will be permanent over time.

> **Successful turnarounds are all about getting commitments to do things differently.**

A CEO who is new to the organisation will also inevitably find with the turnaround process that some of the senior managers will not be prepared to become totally committed to the process. This could occur any time and inevitably there are some that the new CEO might feel are just 'holding their breath' to see how things will go before committing. Unfortunately, these non-performers need to be removed in order that the CEO will be able to demonstrate his commitment to high performance for the company, and that the team that he chooses to work with is one that he could trust. In some instances, new CEOs bring in some of their old colleagues who they have worked with in the past, with the rationale that they are a 'known commodity' for their ability to perform and be trusted. This should always be carefully executed in order not to be accused of 'cronyism'. Whist the CEO may have seen their performance and trustworthiness in the past, the rest of the managers and employees at the current company have not. Performance is demonstrated through actions and results; trust is built over time. Don't exert your 'corporate managerial will' inappropriately – give others time to see and know what you have seen and come to know.

Organisational restructuring deals with the human elements of face value, pride and emotion. This point cannot be over-emphasised and, consequently, it is important to begin the implementation of a new structure with care, sensitivity and fairness. Executed properly, it will produce a workforce that is enthusiastic, motivated, dedicated and committed, and the achievement of the objectives of the vision will be significantly smoother.

Business processes

The business processes are the way the company conducts its business and through which the company is managed. Most companies will have seen the creation of all kinds of procedures, forms to fill in to manage the customers' orders, the requisition for raw materials, packaging, engineering spares, extension of leashes etc, documentation for raw materials, intermediates and final products testing, personnel information, expense claims and the list goes on and on. While some of these are no doubt required for effective and efficient operation of the business, it can be very helpful to audit the numbers of procedures, systems and forms and critique its usefulness. And the beginning of a turnaround effort is the best time to do this.

When looking at businesses processes, two things are important. First, which processes are key to ensure that a business can successfully operate its core business; and second, which of these processes do not contain duplication or wasted efforts. Identifying the key processes can be a bit political, as 'process owners' will strive to have the process they are responsible considered to be key. Most organisations have between six and nine key processes – the important words here are 'key processes'.

A key process is one that contributes to the successful operation of the business *and* generates revenue. The real test for identifying which processes are key is to match them up on a matrix with the needs of your customers. Any process that does not meet the needs or your customers and contribute to revenue acquisition doesn't count as a key process. According to this definition, the finance functions processes are clearly important, but not key. Yes, without the process of invoicing clients for products and/or services, a business would probably not have a stable cash flow, but customers really don't care about getting invoices; they care about receiving the products and/or services that they want and need. And finance processes do not *generate* revenue; they ensure that it comes in, but they do not generate revenue. Production for manufacturers, research for pharmaceutical companies, and customer service for all companies are, however, key processes. When identifying your company's key processes, work to avoid the political pressures that will almost certainly surface – six to nine, that is what there usually is for most businesses, which probably includes yours.

> Key processes are those that contribute to the successful operation of a business and generate revenue.

The issue of wasted efforts is rampant in organisations today. Here is an example of typical waste found in processes. A CEO giving a seminar explained that when he joined a company in which a key processes was the sales function, one of his first ventures out of the office was with a company sales representative. On this trip, he noticed that the sales representative regularly took time off to fill in a series of forms detailing the time he spent with the customer, who he talked to, what was discussed and any orders taken, the mileage he travelled to see the clients, his parking charges and any other expenses he incurred for the company. By the time he finished filling in all these forms after each visit it did not allow him to conduct more than four client visits a day. The amount of details required was hampering his potential effectiveness and the CEO immediately realised why the Sales Manager had put in a request for several additional sales representatives. The processes of the company stated that the sales representatives had to turn in all this information each week, with the intention being that the information would be a benefit to the company. And if that were not enough, each of these forms needed to be signed off by the sales representative's immediate superior at the end of the working week. The representative's expenses needed to be counter-signed by the superior of his superior. This story is a good example of how the best of intentions can sometimes run amuck. This was a case of processes that not only were not beneficial, they were also not providing any return on the investment of time and effort – not to mention the impact on the sales representative's morale.

The CEO immediately instructed the accounting department to pull all sales representatives' expenses over the last 18 months and found that the amount was less than US$100 per month as the car and petrol were provided by the company. He converted this amount into an allowance after inflating it by 20 per cent and promised to index it against inflation. Similarly, the CEO held a meeting with his senior sales personnel and simplified the forms. The end result was that the accounts and sales administration departments freed up four staff members owing to the lack of work and the Sales Manager was convinced after three months that he no longer needed the additional four representatives. The immediate impact on the sales process was dramatic – a re-energised sales force that wasn't confronted with impediments to their real activities of getting business for the company, impediments in the sales process that caused lost motivation and an inability to hit the targets that they were challenged with.

The information retrieval function tends to be ripe with overlaps and wasted efforts as well. How often does it happen that when a new computer program is required to assist in a more effective way of conducting business, to be told that the IT system can no longer handle the additional load. If an audit were undertaken it would ascertain that a large percentage of all the computer reports that are routinely processed were written and required a long time ago and no longer had any relevance. However, it is more than likely that no one has bothered to informed the IT department to cease printing. In the end all these factors inevitably create bureaucracy, prolonged decision making, demotivation and frustration in the workforce – all elements that are non-conducive to a lean, effective and efficient organisation.

If the internal systems and procedures are inefficient, it is also very likely that customer service, order processing and planning, manufacturing, distribution and invoicing, in fact the whole supply chain is most probably in the same state. A lot of computer programs have been written on a customised basis when they could be bought straight off the shelf with some modification. This would not only simplify the process of information retrieval but will also improve transparency, effectiveness and efficiencies.

It is not uncommon for many companies to experience improper and sometimes deficient information on the profit levels of products and services. At times companies might only report contributions of these products and services with profitability at the overall company level as opposed to being identified per product and/or per service supplied. This allegation might seem surprising but is present in a lot of companies. By not identifying profitability per product and/or service, it is impossible to make key decisions about which product or service is worth keeping or growing. Every effort should be put forth to get this information to price the company's products and services profitability, or to delete non-profitable lines. This task is most important if the strategic vision is ever to be realised. A case in point is the achievement of sustainable high levels of profitability of an SME in the London area. The prime issue at the time was the lack of profitability in the UK market in several product lines, and to turn it around, information relating to the profitability of products at customers' level was required. In the past, the information that was available only dealt with overall contribution levels. After an effort was put forth to identify the various products' profitability, management was able to specifically target products for price increases that assisted in being able to deliver a successful turnaround of performance.

Managers today need to realise that being responsible for process decisions is an ongoing, full-time job in itself. Optimising processes does not happen easily, and it is not a one-time job. Process optimisation should be considered to be something that is explored constantly. This does not imply that a manager must spend hours each day doing it, but it does mean that process optimisation should occur whenever there is a better way to accomplish something. This also means that managers should look to their employees to get their input as to how best to optimise a process.

Operators who do the work probably know more about how to optimise processes than the managers who sit in offices.

In a mid-west American manufacturing company, the processes and their accompanying process steps had been identified by two senior managers. While their intent was good, they had little or no experience in actually *doing* the processes and, consequently, the process steps that they had identified were flawed. This resulted in wasted time, wasted efforts and wasted resources – all in the name of 'following the process'. The best way to correct this – this is what those managers eventually did – was to go out into the factory and ask the employees charged with delivering the processes if there was a better way to get the job done. The results were astonishing – reductions of 30 per cent in time required to deliver a process was not uncommon and, with it, a corresponding reduction in costs associated with the process. Asking employees for input has multiple benefits when looking to optimise processes. First, if there is an easier and better way to do it, the employees (the ones who do the process day in and day out) know. Second, the fact that the employees are being asked has knock-on benefits from a motivational and commitment standpoint. Employees feel that their input is valued and their willingness to contribute increases. This can reap massive benefits during a turnaround effort.

Another malice that most companies fall into is the number of meetings held and the large number of participants. Meetings are important and the forums are good to get issues resolved, plans reviewed and approved and decisions taken. For any meetings, participants should only be invited on a basis of 'a need to know and ability to contribute' and with an overriding purpose of 'gainful employment'. Another issue of decision making is that all companies should have a documented authority limit for both budgeted and non-budgeted items and should be noted over certain levels by senior management and, if appropriate, with the Board. If a manufacturing facility is involved, a systemic approach should be adopted for expenses, especially with maintenance expenditure and capital expenditure where lines could be blurred. Not getting them right would not only impact on the depreciation and other financial ratios, which no doubt will be used to monitor progress, but also could lead to abuse.

All businesses have processes. And it is the processes that allow the business to function and, hopefully, function profitably. By examining which processes are key to the profitable functioning of the business, an organisation has a better chance to realise its vision, and its potential.

Human resource architecture

When one looks at an organisation, it is inevitable that part of the examination should focus on the organisation's most important asset – its people. The people who comprise an organisation are the vehicle that enables it to operate effectively, to generate the products or services that it offers, satisfy the customers' needs, which will lead to repeat business, all of which will generate the revenue and its profits. In essence without people, there is no business.

If the human resource of a company is motivated, dedicated and innovative in their quest to gain business at the most effective and efficient ways compared to its competitors, we have the foundation for a profitable business. However, if the human resource is substandard, lethargic and non-dedicated, the business will not be operating at its optimal level and ultimately will generate losses, not profits. Getting the right people in the right jobs, giving them the right training, is not only essential, it *is* the business.

Here is a example which shows that by getting the human resource element right, you can have a financially sustainable business. This is one of the key success factors in supporting the other elements of the corporate turnaround vis-à-vis the organisational structure, business processes etc. It is the factor that will deliver the objectives, targets and milestones of the strategic vision.

> **Human resource practices have contributed nearly 10 per cent to bottom-line financial performance – more than double the figure five years ago.**

Traditionally, the function of human resources departments has shifted from primarily industrial relations to personnel administrations and now to strategic HR management. A recent study by the University of Michigan Business School found that HR competencies and practices had an impact on nearly 10 per cent of business financial performance, more than double the influence of five years ago. However, this measure might be conservative if one takes into consideration the variables of the skill levels of employees, the effectiveness of business processes and organisational structure. These variables, combined with the right working environment, can substantially improve productivity and product or service quality.

HR departments have a large part to play in ensuring that the new structure has the right 'horsepower' to ensure that the right people are in place to get the best 'blend' of people and skills to move successfully toward the strategic vision. A proactive HR department should not only have a good understanding of all the dimensions of the vision, but also the likely impact on the organisation in terms of skill sets required for both the near term and long-term. To do this, HR personnel should work closely with the key managers to define their needs and assist in identifying 'promotables' and 'high potentials', and to put programme in place to realise the individuals' potential for the good of the company.

Quite often these individuals – the high potentials – are extremely marketable and if the opportunities do not exist within the company, the organisation may risk losing them to competitors. An effective HR programme should form part of the succession planning processes. The ability to ensure that appropriate people are ready to take on new challenges is crucial for sustainable success. Without this ability, performance gaps can develop quickly if a key manager takes ill or decides for some reason to move on. Of course, not all departures from these positions are always predictable but the ability to minimise them will bring less disruption and upheaval.

> **High potential employees are highly marketable – if you don't find opportunities in the company for them, another company will.**

To be more strategic and thus cause senior people to not be required to 'pick up the slack' due to performance gaps, it is quite common today for HR departments to outsource the traditional areas such as payroll administration and transaction processing. Additionally, call centres can be set up to answer staff queries about human resource issues, while intranets can provide 'self-service' online access to allow staff to sign on for training courses, check on outstanding leave balances or identify potential internal job vacancies.

Traditional functions of an HR department, such as screening employment applications and new employee induction processes, should be kept intact (although reviewed for effectiveness). Part of this can be as simple as making sure new employees are shown the physical layout of the company, i.e. where the lunch room is, where their peers work and who they are, where environmental health and safety areas are, and what to do in an emergency. These traditional functions of the HR department should always be preserved, especially if the right kind of culture is to be enhanced.

Quite often, during the interview process, new hires are told that the company is a 'caring organisation' but once they actually begin their work, they find out that all that matters is 'getting the job done, regardless'. It is important that an HR department should free itself up for strategic tasks but it should never forget its traditional role – to help the company to look after its most important asset so that the employee feels that their existence is valued and in turn feels motivated to give their best.

It is not always possible to anticipate all the needs of a new employee, especially in the today's global business environment. A Singaporean-based UK pharmaceutical manufacturing facility developed a 'buddy' system to deal with this potential problem. This system involved assigning an existing employee to the new employee for a period of time to act as both a 'new hire mentor' and an organisational 'guide'. The HR department arranged periodic interviews of both the new hires and existing employees, individually and collectively, to seek their views of the general well-being of the new employees. This process also enabled the HR department to ascertain how the system could be improved. Interestingly, after this system was introduced, the turnover rate was reduced to half (if one takes away the departures owing to better and higher grade positions, or significant salary increases). This was a significant benefit to the company as the demand for competent, qualified employees has escalated over the past years.

Another crucial function of a HR department is to ensure the competitiveness of the company's emolument/remuneration packages, including its incentive and bonus policies. Not all employees expect the company to be the best payers but they need to be assured that the compensation they receive is competitive. This should include non-cash benefits such as health care and other social welfare items.

Creating the right environment with the right kind of incentives – security of employment and training and advancement of skills, cohesiveness of the workforce, empowerment, clarity in the financial health of the company, and ability to speak one's view with no fear of recrimination – will greatly assist in getting the workforce to support the turnaround effort and ultimately the achievement of the strategic vision. The ability to ensure that the workforce of an organisation 'feels' that they are supported with both challenges and an effective human resource infrastructure is a key element in any organisation's journey toward its vision.

Organisational culture

Too often, the culture of an organisation is believed to be just something that happens, and that has little impact on the success of the organisation. Well, it does 'just happen', but it happens for reasons. And unfortunately, quite often, the reasons that are identified are in reality just symptoms of underlying issues driven by the dynamics of how the organisation is run. High performance is a function of committed people, ability to execute to a plan, and a positive organisational culture.

> **People + execution + organisational culture = performance potential.**

Creating and cultivating an organisational culture that is conducive to delivering consistent, sustainable high performance is not only time consuming but can also be quite difficult. Changing from a closed, restrictive, non-motivational culture can take up to two years or more. But this time can be prolonged if there is a new CEO and/or the company is undergoing massive change brought about by a turnaround effort. This effect can be further compounded by:

❑ Some managers and senior managers who are not totally committed to the changes required by the turnaround.
❑ The removal of staff whose skill set no longer matches those of the new organisation.
❑ Recruiting externally, especially recruiting managers who may have worked previously in other organisations with the CEO.

Additional cultural issues that arise when working to turn around performance effort include:

- Perceived ability to shift behaviours.
- Existing business pressures – fires that need to be put out.
- Reactive thinking.
- Time pressure.
- Perceived ability to contribute.
- Perceived level of complexity.
- Preconceived mental models.
- Clarity around expectations.
- Clarity around processes.
- Alignment of vision and capabilities.
- Level and intensity of organisational defence mechanisms.
- Perceived effectiveness of processes and systems.
- Perceived appropriateness of processes and systems.

All of these issues need to be dealt with to shift the culture to one that is conducive for a successful turnaround effort.

The thing to remember when working to improve an organisational culture is that 'performance behaviours will get worse before they get better'.

This 'rule' applies to all behaviours. When we learn a new skill, our 'performance behaviour' goes down before it goes up. This is because part of learning a new skill requires that we 'unlearn' old habits. The same holds true for an organisational culture. Being in an environment in which there are examinations of past practices, systems and procedures, as well as performance, can cause employees to become reticent to commit quickly to a turnaround effort. Quite often, what is seen is compliance, but what is really going on under the surface is the application of defence mechanisms on the part of managers and employees who are, to put it mildly, terrified of what may happen next. To prevent this dynamic from draining the turnaround effort, a comprehensive communications plan needs to be put into place.

A comprehensive communications plan should identify *and make clear* why the company is undergoing the turnaround effort, how it will do it, what the employees can expect during the process, and what the company *and its employees* will gain from the effort. The plan should result in a communications roadmap – a path to follow to ensure that all employees, regardless of level or location, know what is going on, for what reason, and how it will occur.

> **A sound communications plan can provide clarity around why the company is undergoing change, how it will do it, what the employees can expect during the change, and what can be gained from the effort. It can make or break the turnaround effort.**

It is highly advisable that the CEO is the principle person to give this presentation *in person*, and as often as possible. If logistic problems preclude the CEO from appearing, then a video presentation should be used with the CEO giving these messages, along with handouts that address the most frequently asked questions relating to the turnaround effort. If the CEO is not able to deliver the communications in person and a video is used, then a senior manager should be present. And clearly, the senior manager should be not only well versed in the message and willing to listen to the concerns of the audience, but he (or she) should be one who is fully committed to the effort.

It is helpful for regularly scheduled follow-up sessions to be offered. Remember, the main purpose of the communications plan is to make sure that concerns of employees are dealt with in an open and honest manner, and if employees think that management is 'keeping something secret', then their defence mechanisms will turn on and the ability to succeed with the turnaround plan will die a rather dismal death. Any comments or queries should be noted and answers or replies required should be given as soon as possible. Be open and honest and if an issue has not been considered, then respond honestly that it was not identified previously and would be taken into consideration immediately. And then do it. Quite often, it is the front-line employees who have the best insights as to the pitfalls of a change effort; after all, they have probably been through more than one. Remember the success of the turnaround is dependent on the buy-in and support of all staff. The more one could convert to the necessity of the turnaround, the fewer employees there will be who are undecided and uncommitted.

This is a very critical stage in a turnaround effort. A new CEO will be the target of efforts to gain his respect and admiration. This can result in managers and/or staff believing that they need to tell him what they think he wants to hear, which may not be the reality of what is really going on. This dynamic is a symptom of an organisation that is riddled with fear. And over time, an organisation that operates in a fear environment will see a decline in motivation, innovation and the ability to work collaboratively. And this environment will cause a turnaround effort to fail and, with it, the company.

A new CEO once told a seminar that in the first month after he was brought in to initiate a turnaround effort, he was walking with a manager through the corridor of the factory, and walking in the opposite direction were two machine operators. When they were close to the CEO they stepped aside with their backs to the wall to allow the CEO and the factory manager through. This was not an issue of showing respect, nor was it an issue of a narrow corridor. The CEO discovered that the environment up to that time was one in which operators were only supposed to communicate 'upwards' in the organisation through hierarchical channels. He knew that he would never be able to gain the operators' commitment unless they felt that he was the right person to lead the turnaround effort, so the next day, he went back to the factory and sought them out. And they talked . . . and he listened . . . and won them over.

The CEO needs to get out of his office and get onto the shop floor to meet the employees, to ask questions and, most importantly, to listen to what is said. Engaging employees – shop employees, office employees, cleaning employees, truck drivers, union members, non-union members, all employees – is the only way to find out where their concerns are, answer their questions, and get their input as to how to make the company a better place to work.

> **CEOs and their direct reports need to lead by example, not by mandate.**

When considering how to ensure an organisational culture that is conducive to a high-performing company, society cultures must be examined. Reverence to authority – an integral component of Oriental society where the Confucianistic upbringing and education teaches one to be respectful for the elders and also someone in authority – is a case in point. There was an incident in a British Singaporean-based pharmaceutical factory where the Director of Quality brought a problem to the new Technical Director who had recently been seconded from Australia. The first thing out of the mouth of the Director of Quality was 'there is a problem'. After he explained the nature of the problem, he was quiet and the Technical Director asked what was his recommendation to fix the problem. Surprisingly the Director of Quality responded that in this business relationship, as the Technical Director was his superior – this shows the impact of societal culture in which the quality manager was raised – he should be the one tell him the solution and then he (the Director of Quality) would go to implement it. The Technical Director responded that this was not the culture he intended to cultivate, he wanted an open discussion of the pros and cons of the solution he brought forward and collectively they would make the decision. As the Director of Quality did not have any solution in mind he was sent away to think about the issue and to come back when he had one. This incident reverberated throughout the factory and interestingly some of the direct reports of the Technical Director liked the new style, while some were not sure of how to take it at all.

Over time, the Technical Director was able to win over most of his direct reports to this new open communication style and when the Technical Director was made Managing Director of the business he was able to turn around (with a strategic vision developed) the operation with a cost reduction of some 50 per cent. He could not have done this on his own, and he knew that the only way he could have achieved those gains in performance was to have an open, collaborative environment in which the other managers and employees recognised that their input was valued.

CEOs – and their direct reports – need to lead by example. Demonstrating a genuine concern for employees and the future of the company will be seen and recognised by the workforce. A CEO must be seen to be fair, just and trustworthy if he wants to create an open and trusting culture. He needs to use any opportunity that presents itself to reinforce his commitment and while it might be time consuming, getting it right will enhance the ability of the organisation to realise and achieve the goals of the turnaround.

Technological innovations

The *Collins English Dictionary* defines 'technology' as:

1 The application of practical sciences to industry or commerce.
2 The methods, theory and practices governing such applications.
3 The total knowledge and skills available to any human society for industry, art, sciences, etc.

Likewise 'innovations' is defined in the dictionary as 'something newly introduced, such as a new method or device'. Whether it is products, services or methodology in business processes, an organisation needs to continue to innovate to stay in tune with the ever-changing market conditions and the taste of customers with its products or services. The purpose of this is clear – it is to stay viable.

Technology is evolving so quickly these days, if an organisation does not follow quickly, there is a great risk that the company is likely to be left behind. Think of some of the technological innovations that we have seen put into everyday business use in the past 25 years: communications were greatly enhanced with the advent of the fax machine; mobile phones have gone from thousands of dollars to just dollars; email has become the medium of choice for both 'letters' and the transmission of documents. One of the latest advancements in technology is a combination of mobile telephone and email – a way to send and receive email away from a hard-wired computer terminal. And the prices for all of these systems keep falling faster than the New Year's ball in Times Square. It all makes you wonder where we will be in the next 25 years.

While communications technology has advanced at a rapid rate, business process technology has seen many innovations as well. Take the issue of the supply chain. To be cost effective and efficient, a company needs to have systems and procedures in place that keep track of the flow of the raw materials so that products at every stage of their conversion and through the distribution network have a significant advantage over those companies that still rely on the manual system to keep track of their inventory.

Inevitably a superior system such as the one just described will have rather low inventory, fewer rejects and hence less handling. This will result in lower required working capital. Low required working capital not only conserves cash but also lowers the cost of borrowing.

In a British pharmaceutical factory based in Taiwan, the CEO implemented a 'computer integrated manufacturing' system for his factory that converts raw chemical ingredients into tablets, capsules and injections at an enormous cost. This system has the ability to pinpoint batches of products that do not meet specifications at the stage of manufacture rather than waiting until the end of production to see which products will meet compliance specifications. The net result was a reduction of product rejection of 3.5 per cent of sales per year. This is significant, especially compared to its competitors who were unprepared to make such investment. And a side benefit of the system was that management was now able to make better decisions *and* use the savings for reinvestment.

> **Patents are little protection from an innovation-driven competitor.**

The effective application of innovative technology is the vehicle with which management can make better decisions. Products and services need to be reviewed in the context of their life cycles and competitiveness in the market. We need to remember that in today's marketplace economy, current specialty products (which command higher prices and, hence, higher profits) are tomorrow's commodity products. In this type of environment, better decisions through innovation can be a salvation. This applies to companies with ten employees as much as it does to companies with 10,000 employees.

Even in the pharmaceutical market, a new drug, which was protected by patent, would only enjoy five years of exclusivity in the 1990s before a 'me-too' or superior performance competitive product would be introduced. The 'exclusivity' time factor is decreasing due to new innovations in chemical compounding, which are able to bring new solutions to existing problems. The process of innovating and launching new compounds is time consuming, however, the time to market has shrunk from ten years in the 1990s to approximately seven years today. And it will be less tomorrow.

Having a competitive advantage through the use of innovative technology enables a company to gain market share quickly, and with new product exclusivity protected by patents, massive research and development costs can be recovered along with an acceptable profit path that ensures future growth for the length of 'protected' time.

Technological innovations can enable a company to sustain competitive advantage and potentially create entry barriers for competitors. Competitive advantages can increase the probability of high performance of the company through the achievement of the objectives, targets and milestones of the strategic vision.

A case study well documented by Harvard Business School in the late 1980s demonstrates the methodology used by Otis elevators to sustain its competitive advantage and its financial viability for many years. In the elevator market, installations of new elevators are not high profit generators due to competition in the marketplace.

Otis came up with the idea of installing a small computer at the back of the elevator to monitor its key operating functions. Tight tolerances are required for elevator operation, and when any of these tolerances were reached, it would trigger a signal by the computer. The signal would be transmitted via a telephone line to a monitoring centre. This centre would immediately be able to identify the elevator, the building and where it was located. A message would then be sent to the nearest Otis maintenance centre, which in turn would print out a 'job order'.

The service personnel would then attend to the correction of the fault before the elevator broke down. This is true preventive maintenance and hence a technological innovation that turned into a competitive advantage and removed an entry barrier. This system is now incorporated into automobiles where a diagnostic kit is plugged into the engine of an automobile and a printout will ascertain the faults and what parts need to be replaced to get the vehicle to perform at its optimal level. In some vehicles, when the faults are detected, a signal is transmitted via satellite to the nearest service centre. These examples show how innovative technology can create competitive advantage for companies – competitive advantage that can mean the difference between survival and going out of business. And when a company has this type of competitive advantage, its ability to be turned into a profitable company increases dramatically.

Too often, however, the knowledge of both the potential competitive advantage and how to use it effectively, are lost due to the level of pressure on management to keep the company alive. When this occurs, potential competitive advantage can evaporate, allowing additional pressure on the company and its management team.

The most important asset any organisation has is its people. And it is their ability to use technology to develop innovative processes, procedures, products and services that can solidify differentiation in any marketplace.

The reality is that, due to the fact that the world of business is complex, and that businesses comprise people (often with the best of intentions), it looks and acts like the graphic shown below.

For those of you who are thinking to yourself that this looks too chaotic and messy, well, this is the way things are. Whilst it is possible to draw nice, clean circular diagrams of how a business is

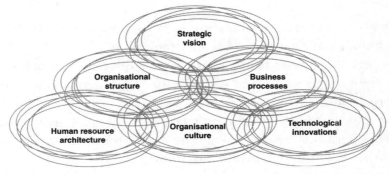

Figure 37

supposed to work, the reality is that it really doesn't function that way. There is no 'right' or 'wrong' in making business decisions – decision making is not like mathematics where you can prove that something is 'right', i.e. the square root of 625 can be proved to be 25. Business decision making is far more situational – the right decision today is really just the 'best decision' based on the current situation, what is known, and what the options are. And consequently, the entire process of turning around a non-performing business can look and feel a bit chaotic at times. It should also be recognised that performance behaviours will get worse before they get better, so any ideas (or hopes) that turning around business performance can be a 'quick fix' should be abandoned before you read any further. Turning around business performance is hard work. It requires a clear picture of what you would like the organisation to look like in the future, and it requires commitment to make that picture reality. The bottom line is that an effective turnaround effort requires the right blend of people, execution, and being willing to not get ahead of yourself. The following is a story that tells just how this was done.

Phoenix Corporation

The situation

Phoenix Corporation is similar to many organisations today. It was founded in the early 1980s and from the start, several members of the same family have run it. From rather humble beginnings, it grew quickly, with the funding largely coming from external sources.

As the company grew in both revenue and scale, it grew as well in debt, with the debt becoming one of the drivers for additional growth – only through continuous growth did the family ownership believe that it could sustain the ongoing debt pressure.

And grow it did, but after about 15 years, it had a serious impediment to the growth process.

By 2000, Phoenix was global, but in name only. It had sales offices and business units in Asia, Europe and North America. That was the good news . . . the bad news was that the business units rarely talked to each other, there was no integrated planning process, shared services were spotty at best, and the business unit directors each had different agendas that they were driven by. The only messages that came from the home offices were to grow and to grow faster. Growth requires stability, and Phoenix was anything but stable. Phoenix's founders were keen to become big in the process control industry, and by the turn of the 21st century, the industry was oscillating wildly. Raw material costs were fluctuating wildly due to the petroleum sector, and many seemingly 'stable' products were fast becoming commodity driven. The potential to consistently grow was becoming harder and harder, and with this and its mounting debt, the company was finding itself in serious trouble. While Phoenix's senior management team viewed itself as running a sustainable global business, there was little chance for this to occur unless something was done.

It was decided that in order to turn the company performance around, a new person should be brought in – brought in meant from the outside, i.e. a non-Phoenix person. The rationale was correct – hire someone who could bring a new perspective to the business, and with this new perspective, pull the various business units together to stabilise the environment and flatten out some of the oscillation that the company was suffering from. After some searching using their paternalistic network, the company hired an external person who had turned around quite a few businesses in the past. It was interesting that they were looking for someone from the process sector who could demonstrate real leadership. This is interesting because, while most organisations in this situation tend to search out help from the same business sector, turning around a business requires high competency levels of leadership, not technical expertise. Phoenix was lucky – they found someone who not only had substantial experience in the process sector but also had high-demonstrated leadership competencies.

After coming onboard in early 2001, the new CEO quickly set out to sort out where the company was and what needed to be done. Before the new CEO was hired, he had spoken to the Board of the business to see what they saw the challenge as. He was told the part about the money slipping away, but at the same time, he was not given a reason for this occurring. As a matter of fact, there seemed to be little understanding even of how fast the money flow was going the wrong way. Clearly, the CEO would have to do some exploratory work to sort out the differences between the symptoms of the problem – what the Board told him – and the underlying causes for the situation the company was in.

The findings were not surprising – the process sector is pretty incestuous and the Phoenix situation was not a secret. The company was haemorrhaging cash at a frightful rate. It had a negative cash flow and was, due to the way the separate business units had been run, highly politically driven. The company did, however, have potential – it had solid assets in some areas, it had a good grip in some markets, and it had a strong research and development and manufacturing capability in some areas. On the surface, Phoenix was a perfect turnaround target.

The complications

Phoenix had three existing cultures driving behaviours in its business. The different cultures were a function of the fact that the company had grown through acquisition, and with each acquisition, it not only possessed new assets, new capabilities and new markets, it was also saddled with additional cultural 'baggage'. In many cases, assimilating a new culture into an organisation can be difficult work, but in the case of Phoenix, hardly any assimilation effort was put forth. New acquisitions were simply added to the roster of companies under the Phoenix banner, and were then permitted to continue with business as usual; with the minor exception that financial contributions were to be sent to the home office. But other than that, it was business as usual.

The three prevalent cultures were different. One North American business culture of Phoenix was epitomised by a mental model of 'operating massive facilities to full capacity', regardless of stated or perceived customer needs. The Australian business culture was epitomised by a mental model of 'focus on customers' needs at the appropriate pace and requirements'. And the last major cultural element, their European business unit, was epitomised by a mental model of 'everyone for themselves'. Europe's business was divided into subsets of 'country-based' businesses, with each country doing what they felt that they should do for their own customer bases. No shared services, no shared or coordinated sales or marketing efforts, no shared or coordinated manufacturing. The only business element that did have some semblance of 'sharing' was the European R&D group, but it was not shared well. Sharing was based on power demands from individual country management and not on customer needs.

The fact that there were mental models – and consequently structures and actions – at play that were different in the three

	Europe	Asia	N. America
Centralised sales force	no	yes	yes
Centralised marketing	no	yes	no
Centralised R&D	no	yes	no
Centralised manufacturing	no	yes	no
Centralised decision making	no	yes	no
Coordination with other regions	no	no	no

Figure 38

main business regions meant that the potential of the organisation was not being realised. It was the mental models that contributed to the decisions as to how to run each business unit.

In Figure 38 it is clear to see that 'centralisation of efforts', i.e. the coordination of decision making, was different in the regions and, in several cases, different based on the decision itself.

In addition to the complications due to cultures that varied across regions, there were substantial external drivers that were causing problems for Phoenix. At the time, the market was highly competitive and costs for petroleum-based raw materials were soaring, with raw materials increasing at an average rate of 4 to 15 per cent. This caused havoc with supply contracts. Most supply contracts were based on six-month timeframes, and with the spiralling increase in costs, by the time contracts could be renewed, they were loss-ridden. As the overall industry was only running at about three-quarters capacity, the ability to press customers too hard was mitigated. Growth for the industry as a whole was negligible, and the strong dollar pre-empted the ability to export from the North American business. And if all these complications were not enough, most western economies were in recession.

Moving forward

Clearly, the challenge of turning Phoenix around was daunting, but do-able. To begin with, the new CEO went back to the Board and talked them through what he planned on doing. 'Talking them through' did not mean asking for permission – the fact that he was hired to turn the company around *was* the permission. What he did was give them an overview of why he was going to do the things he planned on doing. This was an important step in the turnaround process. If the Board was kept in the dark as to what was going to happen, there was a high risk that they would drive and support the organisational defence mechanisms that would normally arise during a turnaround effort.

The Board signed off on the 'plan', but with some reservations. They clearly wanted the company to turn around, but at the same time, they were a bit nervous that they would be losing control over the process. This is always a risk when dealing with family-run organisations. But the choice was not really an option, for if the company had kept going in the direction in which it was going, the rising debt ratio to the lack of positive revenue would have caused the company to be put up for sale, and probably at a 'fire sale' price.

The new CEO brought together the top 12 decision makers in the business. This included senior managers from each region, and the only qualification for being selected to attend was whether they managed a part of the overall business that was adding value. The meeting was a bit chaotic. While the new CEO had provided an agenda, he had also brought in an outside facilitator whose charge was to drive the development and buy-in for a global vision and plan to move the organisation forward. The facilitator and the CEO were conscious that an effective vision and planning process would 'push' the politics and mental models that had kept the company from realising its potential, and they were right.

The meeting began with the new CEO giving a talk about the challenge that the company was faced with, and then the facilitator took over. First, he facilitated the development of a collective vision for the company. The vision was meant to be a description of the company in several years, i.e. if the company would receive an award for excellence, what the award plaque would say. Next, the challenge was to identify all the elements of that vision. The vision was, 'Leadership position in selected markets through supply chain excellence and technology'. In most cases, manager's views on a vision are rather myopic and only touch upon the areas that they believe they can influence directly, and most often look only at what can be readily identified.

The facilitator knew that the greatest challenge of the day would be to get the participants to shift their thinking from 'events' to 'structures'. Events, when speaking about organisations, refer to the easy to see, easily measured things that managers normally focus on. In the process industry, these include revenue, profit, amount of product manufactured and sold, and number of innovations identified and developed. Events are the 'tip of the iceberg' and while they are easy to see and measure, they do not provide high leverage for driving high performance. And in a turnaround process, they are too easy to circumvent. Structures, on the other hand, are the elements that are quite difficult to see, but provide very high leverage for shifting performance behaviour. Structures include both the explicit and implicit policies and procedures that the organisation would follow; stated goals that the organisation would need to attain; physics (what the organisation might actually be able to accomplish); and mental models, how the individual and collective organisational population viewed their world and the organisation they were part of.

Each of the 12 attendees was given a blank piece of paper and asked to identify what they thought the organisation should 'look like' several years in the future. The catch was that the attendees had to identify the future organisation in terms of what events would be seen; what patterns of performance would be seen along the way; what policies and procedures would be needed to drive the patterns (and hence, deliver the events), and what mental models would the managers and employees of the company have to have to get the most out of the policies and procedures (which would drive the patterns, and deliver the events, i.e. business results that would show the turnaround worked). Needless to say, the attendees were not too keen on this, for they had never been asked to think in terms other than end results before. The rationale for this direction was that, if you can get the right structures and mental models in place in an organisation, you would get the results you are after. Less effort, less pressure, less chance of defence mechanisms running amuck, less of everything except results.

The attendees did struggle for a while, but then their thinking began to evolve and they were able to identify each of the required elements. They were then grouped, first in twos, then in fours, and then finally, as one complete group of 12. With each stage of the process, alignment was built and by the end of the day, there was a common picture that all 12 subscribed to – a picture of what the organisation should look like to create success. And the picture provided an opportunity for them to begin to realise what the expectations for their managerial and leadership performance would have to be.

This was an important first step. Without a higher level of alignment that had been present prior to the commencement of the turnaround effort, it was clear that the results that would be shown would be much as they had been, and that would not be good enough to sustain and grow the company over time. Alignment should never be underestimated. Organisations that do not have high alignment, especially at the senior management level, are doomed to fractionalised efforts. Efforts that should be focused on the same objectives can suddenly become adversarial, even though that dynamic is accidental.

Figure 39 shows how an organisation should function – the efforts of business units should support and contribute to the efforts of other business units, the end result being sustainable success for the overall organisation. However, when efforts are not aligned, individual business unit efforts can result in exactly the opposite – a decreased ability to deliver sustainable success and growth.

To counteract this potential, it is important to understand that an organisation under the spectre of change – and a turnaround effort is as dramatic a change as is possible – there are only four types of people; those employees who understand the need for the shift in behaviours and the rationale behind it, and, therefore, support it; those employees who do not understand the

	Desired future reality	Current reality	Gaps or challenges	Action steps	Indicators of progress
Vision *Leadership position in selected markets through supply chain excellence and technology*	We will be a global business that is externally focused to achieve profitability. We will have a harmonised culture with shared values and common goals that are synchronised, but encourages innovation and excellence.	A business defined and operating by region, performing below expectations, lacking common processes and not fully leveraging all its capabilities.	Clarify definitions Global vs. reg. etc. Supply chain Select markets Deliver results Share/exploit technology and knowledge Removing uncertainty Clarity/alignment on common vision Deal with change management Develop common processes		
Mental models *What are the beliefs and assumptions that will be congruent with the vision?*	Change is good. 'We can do it,' belief. 'I understand why?' There is value in diversity. Flexibility Sharing is good. Risk taking is okay to do. Speed, trust, sense of urgency.	No incentive to share. It is 'too hard' to share 'Not invented here.' Uncertainty about who we are, where we are going. Reactive thought process. We are at the mercy of external forces. Lack of alignment. 80/20 rule is okay to use Assess risks	Eliminate uncertainty Create passion, framework Encourage sharing Build/enable pride/ passion Become comfortable with change Use consistent customer focus		

Systemic structures *How can we create structures that will be consistent with those beliefs?*	Knowledge management. Accountabilities Planning, reporting processes Communication plan KPI's, benchmarking Efficient global organisation Reward and recognition programme Career development	Self-contained knowledge Rigid organisation/local structure KPI's undefined No global processes Multiple reporting/measure systems Subjective reward programme Poor communication process Unplanned career development	Need to define R&Rs No common business plan No common organisational plan No process or tools for sharing knowledge Create flexible structure KPIs need to be defined No HR systems No common reporting and planning process
Patterns *What patterns of behaviour do we want the structure to produce?*	Greater number of cross-functional and cross-regional teams working together. Positive trends in rev, contribution, EBIT and other financials. Increased awareness by our customers in selected markets Common business leverage	Regional teams not working together Inconsistent business language Inconsistent business performance Customer is sometimes secondary Willing but . . . Insufficient business communication	Need to do planning collectively Build trust Consolidate strategies Develop consistent knowledge management process Value each other and value customers consistently
Events *Can we describe tangible events that would indicate the vision has been achieved?*			

Figure 39

expectations for change in behaviours and the reasons why; those employees who do not have the needed skills to ensure a successful shift in performance behaviours; and those who simply do not want to change. By surfacing these potential dynamics – as shown in the diagrams – it is easier for managers to identify what could occur and then be able to deal with it. This helps to offset the potential population group that 'doesn't know'. The plan that was the next step in the facilitated process would deal with what skills needed to be installed. The new CEO would deal with the issue of 'those who do not want to change'.

Getting rid of managers who do not want to change in this type of situation can be tricky. Most certainly, managers who do not support and are not committed to a new vision (especially in a turnaround environment) clearly need to demonstrate their unwillingness to change in some other organisation. The tricky part is that probably these positions will need to be filled by someone else. If the organisation does not have other managers who can be moved up to fulfil new and additional responsibilities, the usual action is to bring in new managers from the outside. It is 'tricky' because new managers, regardless of how skilled they are, all have their own 'baggage'. Baggage about how they do what they do; baggage about how they will view the challenge; and baggage about how they interact with an existing team that has a level of 'history' of working together – even if the 'together' is really not that at all.

The additional 'tricky' bit is that if the CEO brings in managers who he has worked with in previous assignments, he may be thought of as sending the signal that he doesn't think that the existing team of managers is up to the challenge and he wants his own team. That doesn't send signals of trust or belief in existing skills or competencies on the part of managers currently in positions in the company, and hence, will mitigate the chance for quick wins that will be crucial for success. In the case of Phoenix, the new CEO only brought in one person; someone who had a skill set that was missing from the existing organisational structure.

The attendees came up with the following mental models – the mental models that would need to be installed to make sure that everyone in the organisation was thinking the same way about both the turnaround and the future of the organisation: Change is Good; We Can Do It; I Understand Why; There is Value in Diversity (of views); Flexibility is Important; Sharing is Good; We Have Pride in Phoenix; Risk-taking is Okay to Do; and a belief in Speed, Trust and a Sense of Urgency. These 'desired' mental models were clearly different than those currently in play in the company: No Incentive to Share; It is Too Hard to Share; Not Invented Here; Uncertainty About Who We Are and Where We Are Going; Reactive Thought Process in Action; We are at the Mercy of External Forces; and Lack of Alignment. When looking at the difference between the desired mental models and the ones in play at the time, it is clear why the organisation was not realising its potential.

Changing the organisational structure

The plan that the participants in the facilitated process formulated pointed out several things: the company would need to change its overall management structure, the new structure would require an interim structure in order to put in place some short-term controls to stop the haemorrhaging, and the team was both up for the challenge and also keen to make it work.

The plan made it clear that the longer-term managerial structure would look like a typical hierarchical organisational chart.

But in order to get there, the plan showed that the interim structure would need to look a bit different.

As can be seen from Figure 41, the need for tighter initial control was identified. Of special interest was the fact that there was an interim position created for integration. The entire situation regarding the existing organisational complexity drove the need to ensure that over time, the organisation would shift

Figure 40

Figure 41

from one in which there were separately controlled business units, and not the belief or effective structure to support a global organisation. The CEO knew that the only way that Phoenix would be able to realise its potential was to make sure that the organisation was truly functioning as one organisation focused on the needs of customers. It was also clear to the CEO that this shift in performance behaviour would not be an easy one.

Shifting organisational performance behaviours usually means that the best path to take is upward. Well, at least that is the way it looks on a graph. But the reality in performance behavioural shift is that performance behaviour will get worse before it gets better. The reason for this is that managers and employees will be faced with not only learning new behaviours, but will need to *unlearn* the behaviours that have not worked in the past. The issue is how to contain the depth and breadth of the behavioural dip.

This effort takes time and while it is happening, performance actually goes down. What is needed when this is occurring is commitment, alignment, support and patience. In the case of Phoenix, the commitment needed to come from the managers and the Board. This was always an issue – how much patience would the Board have? And in the case of Phoenix, the Board's level of patience was not the highest. They wanted results, and they wanted them fast. This was one of the biggest reasons that the CEO chose to go in the direction he did with the turnaround effort. He knew from his previous experiences in turning around businesses that by focusing on the structures that were driving behaviours, he could get more and better results faster.

Something to gain, something to give

To shift performance behaviours relating to processes and technological innovation, it became clear that due to the variance in cultures, different interventions would be required. In the North American business, the prevalent mental models about how to conduct business had prevented the ability to focus as a common sales force and, consequently, reduced the potential to introduce higher value products from the European business. Processes were put into place that would redefine sales territories and introduce technically driven sales training across the global business. Additional processes were identified and installed that would ensure that customers would be able to enjoy the benefits of a rationalised supply chain – a supply chain that would function 'in full, on time, and on specification'.

A new customer service function was installed to act as both the direct contact point for customer issues, and as a way to monitor the effectiveness of both the delivery of products and the collection of revenue receivables. An initial review by the new customer service group was able to identify an account that was overdue for in excess of 18 months, which carried a tremendous cost. The previous financial system had been unable to identify this delay, or the cause of it. By enabling customers to have a 'direct line' to the company, these receivables were able to be collected on time.

An effort was also initiated to determine the profitability of products and customers. While this was very beneficial to drive a focus on which customers to serve that would contribute to the sustainability of the company, and which products to serve them with, this initiative ran afoul with the prevalent mental model to 'just keep all the plants running at full capacity' regardless of profitability. Driving this change in mental models was critical in ensuring that the company would be able to truly 'rise from the near dead' as the company had been headed to. Customers were categorised into three categories. First, those that were deemed to be strategic to the growth of the company, i.e. customers with which potential price increases could have a significant impact on production output. The second category was those customers identified as distributors whose interactions in the past had driven duplications of efforts. The third category of customers was identified as smaller accounts where increases due to the cost of doing business would be passed on. And if this category of customers balked at appropriate increases, they would be discarded. The move to identify and make decisions about product and customer profitability was something that the company had not done in the past, but while it was difficult for managers to get used to – it went in the face of the mental model that all customers were good and should be kept – it was something that needed to be done, and it was another step in shifting the decision making behaviours of the management team.

Procedures were put into place that would encourage the open exchange of information regarding manufacturing, financial decision-making criteria, sales and marketing initiatives and learnings, and research and development – the future of the company – across all three regions. The intent was to instil a mental model of a global business; one in which any component of the business could be brought to bear to help support the company's customers and their needs. This drove the creation of Centres of Excellence – clear demonstrations of organisational best practices throughout the company. To ensure that the

Centres of Excellence were exactly that, an audit was done on the skill sets of each of the 100+ research and development staff in all regions across the company. This also helped in the identification of what skill sets were lacking, and where they were lacking, enabling targeted skill enhancement activities either through external hiring or training.

As the existing computer system that had been in use was unable to provide current and accurate information that would support the newly identified decision making requirements – impact of orders in the system, volume of different products, product mix and profitability v. forecasts – a new system was installed on a temporary basis. The reason for a temporary installation was that, while the activities underway were meant to act to stop the haemorrhaging and stabilise the company, there was no misunderstanding that once the company was solidly on its feet again, an even more powerful system might be needed (which it was).

The European business had some similar process decisions and some that were different than those required for the North American business. The key issue in Europe was the effectiveness of the supply chain and the fact that each country had been run as a private fiefdom. The decision had been made to keep a country-based structure, but to have it function on a pan-European basis. This meant that the managers responsible for country profit and loss, manufacturing and sales would have to begin to talk to each other. These 'conversations' would be key in breaking down existing mental models and behaviours about products and customers. This would be a crucial step forward, as many of the company's European customers were functioning themselves on a pan-European basis. Decisions about product development and extension as well as sales were suddenly not the private domain of a single country manager but instead had to be made collectively. As soon as all the European country managers realised the benefit of decision making sharing, the decision making process actually decreased in time.

Systems were introduced that would allow the collective European management team to review costs of manufacture versus using strategic alliances with competitors. In the past, without the review system, decisions to make or buy were spotty and not consistent, and resulted in excessive costs and, consequently, reduced profits. These decisions were then reviewed on a global basis, enabling the North American and Asia–Pacific businesses to be more closely aware of how they could increase their individual and their collective effectiveness.

Human resource systems were coordinated for the first time. This was for the purpose of enabling specific expertise from one country to transfer easily to another country. While working with an expatriate compensation system that can be more expensive than solely employee 'natives', the benefits from allowing and encouraging transfers – facilitated sharing of expertise and learnings – was well worth the cost.

The Asia–Pacific business had some similarities to the North American and European businesses, and some differences. First, as the Asia–Pacific business was in reality, an Australian business, some of the dynamics and mental models were different. The managers of this business unit had previously run very autonomously – what they did was not impacted by the rest of the world, as they were, just as Australia is itself, quite removed from the rest of the world. But to be part of a global business, it was important that they quickly began to feel part of something that was bigger than just Australia. And the quickest and easiest way to accomplish this was to begin to second some of their managers to other business units. The Australians, perhaps due to their remoteness, had been quite successful on an individual basis in some areas, and the global management team was keen to access that expertise. However, being remote also drove a mental model that was identified in the planning session as 'fierce independence' and it took extra effort to get them to apply the learnings from other regions. But they did, and the benefits were seen clearly, and that drove a willingness to learn more.

The benefits

The turnaround effort of Phoenix did not result in immediate benefits. The term 'immediate' in a business sense is relative, but as the average life of an organisation today is less than one-half of that of a human being (and Phoenix was on a fast decline after only 15+ years), immediacy was an issue. The newly installed CEO drove for both quick wins and sustainable gains. By focusing on shifting the mental models of the various management teams and the structures that needed to be shifted, he was able to accomplish both of these goals.

Strategy and Performance Checklist

The process that I have written about in this book is not meant to be viewed as a 'cookbook' approach. You all know what the cookbook approach is, don't you? You just follow the directions step by step and everything will come out fine. Well, shoot, you know that just isn't the way the world works, don't you? (Don't you? Well, it doesn't). You can use these planning tools and processes as a guide, not as a fixed, cast-in-stone process. After a few times planning in this way, you will know what tool works best for which situation. And the good news is that using this process is like learning to ride a bicycle — you won't really learn how until you get on the bike, so read on.

I know of many organisations that have been able to achieve sustainable high performance by using only parts of this process, and using them in different ways. But the bottom line is that there are several key lessons to be had by incorporating these process steps into the development of an effective strategy and then achieving high performance.

1 **All strategy needs to begin with a vision for the future.** If there is no destination for the organisation to move towards, there will not be any reason for the managers and employees to do anything differently. The vision should be what the organisation would like to be in the next three to five years, and it should incorporate some stretch, yet at the same time, be something that is achievable. Whilst in most cases, visions come from the head offices of an organisation, many times they stem from what the front-line employees see. Be willing and open to listen to the input from all levels of the organisation, as well as to what your customers say.

2 **The vision needs to be complete, and look at all the different dimensions of the desired future.** Visions should include more than just how much money the company wants to make in the future, or what level of market share management wants. A good vision is one that identifies not only the traditionally recognised variables (revenues, profits, market share, etc), but also what patterns of performance behaviour will be visible, what processes, systems, policies, procedures and resources the company will need to have; what kind of working environment the managers and employees will have in the future; and what mental models the managers and employees will have in the sought-after future. If any of these dimensions are missing from the vision 'picture', employees will either assume that these are not considered important by management (a bad signal) or that management is only interested in money (another bad signal). Make sure that the vision is complete, and to do so, ask for input from various levels of the organisation.

3 **The vision needs be communicated clearly to everyone in the organisation, as well as to suppliers and other stakeholders.** Visions that are not communicated effectively – just like any type of communications – set up management for problems that they just don't need. Employees are like any other group of people; when we don't know something, we tend to fill in the blanks with what we think should be there, and in the case of an organisational strategy, that can send mixed signals to employees. And in many cases, these mixed signals lead to mixed and counterproductive actions. Counterproductive actions can become adversarial, and at a time when all organisations are looking to keep costs at a minimum and become more effective with existing resources, internal adversarial relationships can be extremely destructive. Ensure that everyone (managers, employees, customers, and other stakeholders) clearly understand where the company is going, why it is going there, how it will get there, and what will be different when it does finally find itself in the future.

4 **A sound strategy, before it is developed, needs to look at what possible scenarios the organisation may encounter on its journey toward the future.** A strategy that doesn't take into consideration what the future might bring is like going on a non-stop cross-country car journey without a map, or spare petrol, or a spare tire, or membership in the RAC.

Organisations that say that they will deal with future problems if they arise wake up one day with themselves in a mess, and then profess that it isn't their fault . . . which is pure nonsense. One of the responsibilities of management is to make sound decisions that will ensure a positive future for a company; and to do this, they need to be aware of what the future might bring. Sound planning is all about being prepared for contingencies, and if you don't put any effort into knowing what they might be, there is no way you can deal with them before they are all over you. Which, of course, is not good.

5 **Potential scenarios need to be explored to see which of them may prevent or inhibit organisational progress.** Quite often, some of the scenarios that might impact an organisation appear to be negative. Whether it be potential regulatory action, massive competitive pressures, the negative aspects of globalisation, or soaring resource costs, there is the possibility that some of these future scenarios will play havoc with your organisation's ability to realise its potential. Just because you may not like them, it doesn't mean you should ignore them. Even if you believe that the chances of them coming to fruition are low, it is important to explore what you would do if they do occur. Remember the lessons (we should have) learnt from 1974 when the cost of petroleum skyrocketed with the formation of OPEC. Only one of the major energy giants had previously identified this as a possible scenario and, consequently, had a contingency plan in a file, ready to turn on if required. It was required, and they did turn it on . . . and rose to fourth in the energy company rankings. The real lesson is to be ready . . . for anything.

6 **Indicators of progress toward the vision need to be identified before the strategy itself is developed.** Common sense should tell you that anytime you go on a journey, you should know what road signs you will see along the way. If you don't know what the signs will be, there is the chance that you will find yourself somewhere you hadn't planned on going. Make sure that the indicators reflect all the dimensions of the desired future vision. These might include not only what profit levels will be every six months, but also what shifts you will see in the organisational climate, customer retention, and employee alignment and commitment. If you don't currently measure some of these, get started. No measurements, no way to tell how you are doing.

7 **The key indicators of progress should be identified and communicated to everyone concerned, so that they will know what to look for, and what to look out for.**

Tell everyone what you are doing and what they should be looking for. The worst thing for employees is to not know what is going on. I am not saying you have to share confidential business information, but strategies are rarely confidential (if they were, how would anyone know what to do?). If you are concerned that the employees will be disenchanted if progress is not fast enough, the problem isn't how they may feel; it is management's ability to keep progress in line with the plan. You want managers and employees to know how things are going. They want to help, they want to contribute and they, in most cases, have answers and solutions to problems – let them do so by keeping them in the loop. If you choose not to, then be prepared to not achieve your strategic goals.

8 **An initial look should be made to determine how much effort is currently being expended (and progress being made) toward the key indicators.** I have seen many organisations that have been putting massive efforts into activities and/or initiatives that add little or no value to the achievement of strategic goals. This is quite simply a waste of valuable resources. Figure out which of the indicators of vision progress are the most important to look for (you certainly can't watch all the indicators) and then check to see if you are moving toward these at the current time. How much effort are you expending on these in relationship to how much progress you are making. Misplaced efforts, for misplaced results, just is not common sense.

9 **Have a clear understanding about the relationships between what your customers want, and how you go about keeping them happy.** I have seen many examples of organisational management teams that *think* they know what their customers are after, but don't really know. Talk to your customers and, even more importantly, listen to them. Ask them what about your relationship you could change to keep them happier. I don't mean you have to slash prices. Most

customers can deal with costs as long as they receive their component parts and/or services you provide on time, in full, at the necessary quality levels. Just remember, if you don't meet your customers' needs, they will go elsewhere, and then what will you do?

10 **Understand the difference between what your customers *need* and what they *want*.** As a supplier of parts or services, you have several responsibilities to your customers, one of which is to help them sort out the difference between what they think they want and what they really need. And a good way to help them sort this out is to offer to share with them how you do your planning (assuming you do planning effectively). Helping your customers to be successful is the sure way to help ensure your success. Customer supplier relationships are like any other relationship – it takes two to make them work.

11 **Determine what you can do to achieve the organisation's vision. Sort out activities by which ones will provide the greatest leverage, and then sort them by what needs to be done first.** Figuring out what to do should correspond with which indicators are the most impactful. This can be done by using the same set of processes identified earlier in this book. Once you have an idea of all the activities you can do, prioritise them so they reflect where the highest leverage activities are; then take that list and identify which activities should be done first. It makes no sense to put effort into activities that won't get you serious progress, nor does it make sense to do some activities before they logically should be done. Sort out the most impactful activities into years – which ones need to be accomplished in year one, which in year two, which in year three, etc. When you do this, use common sense as the ultimate test.

12 **Understand that when you begin to do the most appropriate activities, there will be unintended consequences, and determine what they might be.** The

whole issue of unintended consequences should not be overlooked. In some cases, the unintended consequences of activities will be good and welcome, but in other cases, they will spell doom to your ability to do what is needed to be done, when it is needed to be done. Use systems thinking cause and effect diagrams to see what will occur when you begin to communicate the strategy, to implement the strategy, and to see the strategy through to completion. Check in terms of your employees' motivation and commitment to support the strategy; the impact on existing resources; your relationship with customers, suppliers and stakeholders; and your ability to realise the potential of your company.

13 **Identify which activities have priority over the other ones.** Priority can mean multiple things: which activities will provide the highest leverage; which activities should be done before others; which activities can be done because of existing but short-term resource availability; and which activities need to be done for legal or regulatory requirements. In some cases, activities go up the priority listing if they take advantage of time-sensitive unintended consequences.

14 **Determine when each activity needs to be done and who should hold responsibility for ensuring that it is done on time.** When laying out the schedule for strategic activities, it is important to ensure that each activity can track back upwards toward the achievement of the vision, and have appropriate timelines for their completion. The timelines that are set need to reflect common sense and should be connected directly to the assignment of resources that will enable them to be achieved on time, in full. Additionally, all the activities need to be connected to a person who will be responsible for their achievement. This does not have to be the person or group who will actually do them, but instead identify one person who will be responsible for ensuring that they are done. Demonstrable proof that they have been achieved also needs to be identified, for without proof of their completion,

there is the risk that they will not be completed on time and in full.

15 **Identify what resources will be needed for each activity and test them with common sense.** Many strategies that I have seen look and sound great, but are doomed to failure because the organisation does not provide the resources needed to accomplish them. Resources that might be needed include people whose time is released from a portion of their existing jobs to work on the strategic activities; funding that will be needed for internal or external spends associated with the strategic goals; temporary support staff to assist in the implementation process; technological support from either internal or external IT organisations; and communications support in order to ensure that the organisation as a whole can be kept informed as to the progress of the work, and to help avoid duplication of efforts of the strategic implementation team.

16 **Figure out what will be appropriate to use as measures for knowing that each activity is completed, and what the tangible proof of completion will be.** Again, use common sense to make sure that the measures and evidence are appropriate. The identification of measures of success need not be a complicated decision. If an activity is to survey customers to determine their level of satisfaction with what products or services you provide, the measure of success is that the survey has been done. It is not that there is a survey; it is not that the customers are happy – if the activity is to do something, the measure is that it has been done. Period. And the logical proof of doing a customer survey, as in this example, is the survey itself. However, if the activity is to increase customer satisfaction, an appropriate measure would be that satisfaction has increased, with the proof being the documented results from customers.

17 **Identify a way in which to audit the progress of the organisation as the strategy activities are being**

implemented. The whole aspect of auditing strategic progress can be far more complicated than it need be and, in most cases, it is. I have always been a big believer in the adage of 'simple is better', and for that reason, would suggest that doing an audit and reporting its results should be as simple as possible. Whilst many organisations seem to like to put out lengthy, multicolour brochures that explain (or think they explain) the status of strategic initiatives, the most logical way to do this is to check with each person who is being held responsible for any strategic activities if they have completed the activity (according to the measure that was set). If the answer is no, then the next question is 'how far are you toward completion?' An answer that you are looking for would be either 25, 50, or 75 per cent done. And the last question you need to ask is 'what can we do to help you stay on time, and on target?' This last question is very important, for it will surface what the person has been up against that may be causing them to fall behind on the targeted completion date for the activity they are responsible for. Once you have this information, the responses should be put into a one-page matrix that identifies what the activities are, what the measure of success and proof is, how much progress has been made, and what additional support is needed (if any). The reason for the one-page matrix is that I don't know of many CEOs who want to, or have the time to, go pouring through executive summaries of multipage PowerPoint reports when all the important information can be placed on one page. With a one-page matrix, the CEO can get an instant view of where the organisation is in making sure that the strategy will come to fruition. Simple is better; common sense is best . . . always.

Some final thoughts: a good friend of mine, and quite often a collaborator on building leadership effectiveness with clients, once reminded me that one of the biggest reasons that the Scottish didn't fare too well over time with the English during the wars of the 1200s was that, whilst they had a brilliant and intimidating way to rush to battle, they were quite often out of breath by the time they reached the opposing armies. This note stuck in my mind and raised questions about why so many change initiatives fail. Is it because the people responsible for the initiative lose track of what they are supposed to accomplish, or are they just exhausted from all the effort they have expended?

Trying to deploy a change initiative — any initiative that will change the organisation or the way the organisation functions — is difficult, and can be filled with obstacles. Some of the chief obstacles are; lack of clarity about what is trying to be accomplished; lack of appropriate resources; lack of staying power; and the potential that the organisation will try to 'reject' the effort. And if it isn't bad enough that some organisations suffer from one of these maladies, there are organisations that suffer from combinations of them. This does beg the question, 'how can this happen?' The answer can be found by looking at some of the challenges organisations and their managements face.

If there are any blinding beliefs in business today, they include, 'get it fixed', 'hit those numbers', and 'get it done now'. These three sometimes unwritten and unspoken commandments drive many business decisions. The implicit message of these commandments is that short-term, myopic thinking is just fine in today's organisational world. And because of it, many management teams seem mired in the same problems year on year.

There are two ways to ensure that an initiative succeeds: drive it, or enable it to succeed. Driving it means . . . well, driving it. Whilst driving an initiative to completion can work, it usually results in marginalised efforts and results, and negative impacts on an organisational culture. However, enabling an initiative to succeed has different results. By enabling an initiative to succeed, managers' efforts are focused on making sure that everyone concerned understands why the initiative is important, both for the organisation and for the people who it will impact, including customers and suppliers — the life-blood of any organisation.

Ensuring that everyone understands the answer to the question 'why', employees can make the connection to their efforts and success. They can see how their contributions lead to that success, as well as understand that their efforts are valued. And because of these reasons, they shift from employees who are compliant (the result of driving an initiative) to employees who are committed.

Part of helping employees 'understand' includes being open and honest about the fact that some employees may be sceptical about the need for the initiative, and the chances of it succeeding. If employees are sceptical, for any reason, their efforts will not be what they need to be, and management is forced into either driving the initiative, or settling for less than desired results. Either option should not be acceptable.

Making sure that employees are aligned behind an initiative may seem like it requires extra effort, and they are right – but only at the preparation stage of the initiative. The overall time – from inception to successful completion – actually is less by investing time up front to make sure that everyone is onboard *before* the actual implementation begins.

index

importance vs. urgency, and the Desert Group case study 112
indicators of vision attainment
  Affinity Process (KJ) 41–6
  Interrelationship Diagraph (ID) 47–51
Influencing
  behaviour 130
  as a core competence 111
information technology (IT)
  and business processes 183
  niche competitors in the IT sector 152
  and organisational structure 178–9
innovation
  and behaviour 130
  and people 39
  and resistance to change 126–7
Institute of Directors 8
intellectual arrogance, and scenario planning 17
internal meetings, communications behaviour in 134–5
Interrelationship Diagraph (ID) 47–51
  and the Arachnid Chart 54, 57
  guidelines for facilitation 51
  header cards 48–9, 52
  and the Matrix tool 69
  process summary 50
  purpose of 50
  and the Tree Diagram 57
  when to use 50

Japanese cars, and GM (General Motors) 4–6
Japanese strategic planning
  Seven Management and Planning Tools (7M&P) 29
  Seven Quality Control tools 28
job descriptions 161–2

key processes 181–2
KJ *see* Affinity Process (KJ)
knowledge, three levels of 23

Ladder of Inference 138–40, 142
leadership
  behaviour 131–8
  as a core competence 111
  Desert Group case study 108–9, 110, 112–13
  and Phoenix Corporation 201–2
  and strategic vision 171
  and vision 40
  see also managers
Leading
  behaviour 130
  as a core competence 111
Left-Hand Column 138, 140–2
Limits to Growth scenarios 75–6
long-term planning 8–10

malaise, organisational 117–18, 119, 121
Management Control Reporting System (MCRS) 160, 161
managers
  and business processes 184–5
  core competencies, and the Desert Group case study 110–11
  improving decision-making 143–4
  managerial behaviour 131–42
    and the Ladder of Inference 138–40, 142
    and the Left-Hand Column 138, 140–2
    matrices 131–8
  measuring performance of 144
  and organisational culture 190
  Phoenix Corporation 210–11
  and strategic vision 171
  and strategy development 32
  see also leadership
manufacturing sector, non or low performers 145–6
maps, and scenario planning 18
market share, and strategic planning 29
marketing, and organisational structure 175–6